Here I am, Lord ...
I know I ain't got no business here
But you said if I ever got so low
I was busted,
You could be trusted

— Paul Simon

Fall seven times, stand up eight

— Japanese proverb

BUSTED BRONCO

From Addiction to Redemption

Joe O'Brien

with Bob Evancho

BooTLEG BOOKS

Great Falls, Montana •
Boise, Idaho • Est. 1996

Published by Bootleg Books
1721 First Avenue N.
Great Falls, MT 59401
(406) 788-0269
joe14obrien@yahoo.com

s**weetgrass**books
a division of Farcountry Press

Produced by Sweetgrass Books
PO Box 5630
Helena, MT 59604
www.sweetgrassbooks.com

You may order extra copies of this book by calling Farcountry Press toll free at (800) 821-3874.

The views expressed by the author/publisher in this book do not necessarily represent the views of, nor should be attributed to, Sweetgrass Books. Sweetgrass Books is not responsible for the content of the author/publisher's work.

Printed in the United States of America

Front cover photograph: Steve Winslow/Winslow Studio
Back cover images: GD Photography (Gracie Duffy-O'Brien)/Wenatchee Valley Venom (top left); Bozeman Daily Chronicle (top right); courtesy of Santa Clara University (bottom)

Front and back cover design: GD Photography (Gracie Duffy-O'Brien)
Interior design: Chris Latter
Copy editor: Sue Evancho

Library of Congress Control Number: 2011911550

O'Brien, Joe
Busted Bronco: from addiction to redemption / Joe O'Brien with Bob Evancho
ISBN: 0-9658911-1-9 ISBN: 978-0-9658911-1-0
1. O'Brien, Joe. 2. Football—United States—Biography. 3. Substance abuse—United States. 4. Drug abuse recovery. 5. Evancho, Bob.

15   14   13   12   11   1   2   3   4   5   6   7

To Gracie
— JO'B

To my sisters and brother
Kate Gladchun
Ann Anderson
Joe H. Evancho
— BE

Acknowledgments

OUR THANKS TO THE FOLLOWING who in various ways provided encouragement and/or assistance to the completion of this book: Joe Aliotti, Barbara Allen Callaghan, Glen Amador, Jim "Kermit" Balch, Tom & Cindy Duffy, Gracie Duffy-O'Brien, Larry Espinola, Joe H. Evancho, Sue Evancho, Mark Freeman, Scott Gipson, Larry Gladchun, Fred Goode, Cliff Hysell, Pete Kwiatkowski, Chris Latter, Sandy Lee, Mike Lefkow, Ron Newberry, Kim Philipps, Sabrina Polidoro, Mike Prater, Jerry Roach, Kelly Roberts, Sam Scinta, Tom Scott, Larry & Sandi Slonaker, Brian Smith, Jerome Souers, Kathy Springmeyer, Jennifer Starks, Ginny Stemler, Bobbie Swingley, Frank Szymanski and Jeff Welsch.

Author's Note

THIS IS MY TRUE STORY.
However, some names have been changed. Events recalled and
conversations retold on the following pages are to the
best of my memory.

Also by Bob Evancho

Pokey: The Good Fight
(with Pokey Allen)

Elegant Soul: The Life and Music of Gene Harris
(with Janie Harris)

Ida Tours the 44: A Book of Idaho's Counties

Prologue

I CALL IT THE LIE. It will be a part of me for as long as I live. It was the 15-year period from my sophomore year in high school until I was busted for possession of methamphetamine in September 2003.

I can't pretend The Lie didn't happen. I can't erase the fact I was a popular and respected college football coach at the time of my arrest. I can't simply push a delete button and start with a clean slate. I did too much damage and disappointed too many people to think The Lie would eventually fade away.

But The Lie does not define me. I won't let it.

I know there are people who feel betrayed by the misdeeds I committed while I lived The Lie—former friends, colleagues and fans who won't forgive me. I can't say I blame them. I tricked them into believing I was someone I wasn't. They point to the serious mistakes I made and the laws I broke. They use words like "convicted felon," and "hypocrite," and it hurts to hear them still.

I offer no excuses and blame no one but myself for my personal struggles, my failures, and the consequences of the poor choices I made.

I thought I could conceal The Lie and keep my drug abuse in check while I continued my love affair with football—first as a player and then as a coach. And for a decade and a half I did a pretty good job. As a high school student in Pittsburg, California, I was a class officer, team captain, most valuable player in three sports, and the recipient of more than 70 athletic, academic and civic awards. I was a well-regarded college football prospect, recruited by numerous schools before I accepted a scholarship to nearby Santa Clara.

In college, my star grew even brighter. I was named the Western Football Conference's Defensive Lineman of the Year as a sophomore. When Santa Clara dropped football in 1992, I transferred to Boise State, earned All-America and Big Sky Conference Defensive Player of the Year honors in 1994, and helped lead the Broncos to the NCAA Division 1-AA national championship game.

But the All-American persona I publicly portrayed as a teenager and young adult belied a troubled and turbulent personal life. I used my people skills and charm to get out of trouble and wiggle out of tight situations.

In high school and college I thought football would eventually deliver me from the abyss and give me the hands-on discipline and structure I often lacked. But it didn't matter; I continued to make choices that took me down a path of dishonesty and self-destruction. I lived The Lie, and it took control of me.

At various times in my playing and coaching careers I was described as a charismatic figure, an inspirational leader on the field, and a huge presence in the locker room. My love for football was pure and genuine, but in reality I was a drug addict, and The Lie had taken over my life. Beneath that veneer of self-assuredness and bravado was an undercurrent of despair, deceit and anger that gripped me throughout much of the first 30 years of my life. Frequently fueled by alcohol and illicit drugs, that anger became an inner rage that was at times out of control.

When I was in college, I could be a brawler. At 260 pounds, I wasn't afraid to throw my weight around. I got into bar fights and scrapes with the law, most of which escaped public scrutiny and media attention. Unbeknownst to those around me, I was using meth and other drugs.

During my brief career as a pro football player I added the drug GHB to my meth use. When my playing days ended I turned my attention to a coaching career in the game I loved, but The Lie was always lurking. After a single season at Northern Arizona I landed a job at Montana State in 2000 as the defensive line coach. I managed to hold The Lie at bay and thrived at the Bozeman school; in early 2003, at age 30, I was promoted to assistant head coach, but people didn't see the entire Joe O'Brien. The personal magnetism and charm I displayed in public concealed my dark secret—one that I continued to keep hidden from my players and fellow coaches.

In Bozeman, my clandestine and illicit behavior worsened. I became involved in a meth ring. After my arrest I was sentenced to four years in federal prison for my role in a drug distribution conspiracy. I served two years and four months and was released in 2006.

My story is one of inner conflict, regrettable behavior, deceit and public dishonor. It's about a tarnished reputation that will take a lifetime to rebuild. It's about surviving, healing and moving on—a story of lessons learned and an inner peace that's now within my reach.

CHAPTER
1

WHEN I WAS AROUND 10 YEARS OLD and living with my dad in Pittsburg, California, I started calling him "Crazy Pops." Given his behavior during the time I knew him, it seemed like a fitting nickname.

Like most kids, I loved my parents, even if they didn't create a nurturing, stable home environment for my three siblings and me. Both my mother and father were part of the California outlaw biker culture (although they were never full-fledged motorcycle gang members) with all its inherent dangers and nefarious activities. My dad died of a heroin overdose at the age of 35 in 1989, a month before my 17th birthday. My mother and I last talked on the phone sometime in 2004 when I was in prison.

As teenagers, both my parents were attractive and athletically inclined with well-proportioned bodies. A strapping 6-foot-2, 225 pounds, Scott O'Brien was the star quarterback and a standout linebacker for the local high school in Pittsburg in the early 1970s. He was also an excellent swimmer, competing at age 13 against the likes of Mark Spitz in events such as the U.S. Junior Olympics. Diane O'Brien (nee Burch), two years older than my dad, was a statuesque track and field standout from Clayton Valley High School in nearby Concord.

Pregnant with me in early1972 at 19, my mother already had a child from a previous relationship; my dad was 17 and a high school senior. Just weeks before his graduation from Pittsburg High School, my dad blew off the remainder of his final semester, spurned offers to play college football, and moved with his pregnant girlfriend and her two-year-old son to Medford, Oregon, where he got a job as a laborer. I was born in Medford on Nov. 6, 1972, joining my parents and my two-year-old half brother Chris. My parents eventually got married and had my sister Autumn in 1975.

Shortly thereafter we returned to their old stomping grounds near Pittsburg, a racially mixed, working-class city northeast of San Francisco, where my dad got a job as a production worker with the paper company Crown Zellerbach. His job paid well but required him to work lots of odd hours.

From the time I began to throw baseballs as a youngster until the day my dad died, sports was our common passion and the bond between us. Despite his sometimes violent and unlawful ways, my father was my biggest influence and most ardent supporter—from my days playing youth baseball through the years that I blossomed into a high school football standout. Sadly, he didn't live long enough to see me play beyond the 12ᵗʰ grade.

Baseball was my first organized sport, and I was pretty good at it. I was actually scouted by the Philadelphia Phillies when I was in high school, and from my Little League seasons through my senior year of high school I was usually one of the better players on the field and a perennial all-star. But my first introduction to sports was football. It all began on a makeshift football field Dad built on our property in Oakley, California, a small town 10 miles from Pittsburg in the middle of California's wine country. He used two oak trees for goal posts and roto-tilled the soil into a level playing field. On his football version of *Field of Dreams* my dad taught Chris, a few neighbor kids, and me the basics of the game.

Not surprisingly, the Oakland Raiders were Dad's favorite team, what with their reputation as a haven for football mavericks, renegades and outcasts. For several years Dad had two season tickets and would alternate between taking me and Chris to the Raiders' home games at the Oakland Coliseum, about 30 miles from Oakley.

Those are some of the good memories, but they are outnumbered by the bad. My parents' marriage was fraught with abuse and violence. They were heavily into alcohol and illicit drugs: marijuana, cocaine, crank—the slang for methamphetamine back then—and Lord knows what else. And they fought, literally, on a regular basis—nasty knockdown-dragouts that had my siblings and me fearing for our safety and running for cover. My parents' brawls were not a mismatch; my dad was big and mean, but at 5-foot-10, 180 pounds, my mother was a tough, nasty, tattooed biker chick who rode her own motorcycle, could hold her own in a fight, and didn't back down from anyone, including my father. And her parenting skills—if you want to call them that—could be similarly violent; if any of her kids stepped out of line, she didn't hesitate to mete out punishment with slaps to the face and belts to the backside that were harsh and painful.

My dad was even more intimidating. Brawny, goateed, long-haired and tattooed, he was a badass on a Harley-Davidson—a dangerous and often violent man with a predilection for gunplay and other criminal activity. It was a perilous lifestyle that caused him to accidentally hit and kill a woman with his car in 1985 while he was under the influence and later cost him his own life 4½ years later when he OD'ed. I make no excuses for my father's many faults, misdeeds and transgressions, but I will say this: He loved his kids.

The only aspect of his life that was as important as his biker activities was his devotion to my athletic endeavors. Throughout the years I played youth and high school sports, he attended as many of my games and practices that his work schedule would allow. With his fluctuating hours at the Crown Zellerbach plant, it was fairly common for Dad to get several days off in a row—a break that often set off a drug and alcohol spree lasting up to three days and requiring an additional day or two of recovery. After one of his benders, one of the few things that would get him out of bed was a game in which I was playing.

MY DAD WAS a complex man. He had a high IQ and could have excelled in a number of professional fields. But he had no interest in a college degree or a white-collar job. Instead, he chose to make his living as a production worker, which was a better fit with the outlaw biker lifestyle he embraced—not that he didn't take his job seriously. In fact, his bosses and co-workers at Crown Zellerbach considered him a productive and reliable employee who was known to work as hard as he played.

But he was truly in his element when "unwinding" with his fellow bikers away from work. And his behavior was often unruly and at times illegal. After one of my freshman football games Dad met some fellow bikers at a local watering hole and proudly regaled them with my latest gridiron exploits. At a nearby table was another patron who had been at the same game. The guy, who didn't know my dad, had been drinking and was loudly criticizing not me, but the play of one of my fellow linemen, Mark Velasquez. *The guy was talking about a game involving 13- and 14-year-olds and he hadn't said a word about me!* But that didn't matter to my dad, who had a short fuse and didn't need much of an excuse to pick a fight or kick somebody's ass.

My dad elbowed one of his companions and motioned to the guy at the other table, who continued his rant about Mark's performance. "Listen," Dad whispered, "I want you to get that asshole out in the parking lot. Tell him you need to give him something, but you can't do it in the bar. I don't care how you do it, just get him outside."

My father's friend somehow convinced the guy to join him outside the bar, where my dad was waiting. Without saying a word he dropped the guy with a direct blow to the face and followed with several kicks and punches as he lay on the ground. I hate to think what Dad would have done to the poor bastard if *I* had been the object of his critique.

GIVEN MY PARENTS' abusive relationship and volatile lifestyle, I'm surprised they remained together as long as they did. The beginning of the end of their already rocky marriage occurred in Oakley in August 1980, soon after my brother—or I should say my *half* brother—Jason was born.

We lived directly across the street from a biker couple (I'll call them Rex and Sheila) and their two kids. My dad and Rex became close friends. They were about the same age, both worked at Crown Zellerbach, and both were hard-core bikers, although Rex was a bit of a pretty boy and not as rough-and-tumble as your typical biker. They partied, got high and rode their Harleys together regularly. When they weren't out riding and raising hell they spent a fair amount of time in each other's garage working on their bikes. Unfortunately for everyone involved, Rex and my mother became quite friendly, too.

As shift workers, my dad and Rex would often work different days and hours, and sometime in 1979 Rex and Mom had an affair. My dad later said he had a sneaking suspicion that there was something going on between them, but convinced himself it couldn't be true—that is until a few weeks after Jason was born.

My dad was there for Jason's birth, and everything seemed fine when my mother and new brother came home from the hospital. But my father's suspicions about Rex and my mom were aroused once again in the ensuing days when it became apparent to Dad that Jason didn't bear any of his physical features.

Putting two and two together, my dad confronted my mother and got her to admit to her affair with Rex. The moment she did, he flew into a rage. "That's not my child!" he bellowed. Grabbing his handgun, a .38 Special, he raced across the street, screaming and wielding his weapon, surprising Rex, who was walking out of his garage. Dad was 250 pounds of deadly fury. He grabbed Rex by the neck, threw him to the driveway, and jammed the barrel of the revolver in his mouth. "YOU MOTHERFUCKER!" he shrieked. "YOU FUCKED MY WIFE AND THAT KID IS YOURS, ISN'T HE?!"

Scared out of his wits and fearing for his life, Rex confessed to the dalliance with my mother. Dad later said he was surprised he didn't kill Rex right then and there. However, knowing their confrontation was taking place in broad daylight, he managed to regain some semblance of self-control. He pulled the gun out of Rex's mouth and walked back to our house, leaving Rex lying and weeping on his driveway. Badly shaken, Rex knew he had literally dodged a bullet. He also knew my father was fully capable of killing him, and he had no doubt my dad would be back—more than likely hopped up on an alcohol- and/or drug-induced rampage. When Shelia found out what had happened she also came unglued and kicked Rex out of the house. "Get the fuck out of here!" she screamed at her husband as he fled out the front door.

Then Rex began to lose it. About a week later in an attempt to evade my dad's wrath, he stole some money, returned to his home, gave the loot to Shelia, and told her to call the police and tell them where he was. After his arrest he was subsequently convicted and sent to prison.

Although he saved himself from my dad, he paid a steep price. Rex was quite handsome but not all that virile or rugged, which can be a bad combination in prison. Years later I found out that Rex had been repeatedly gang raped during the first few months of his imprisonment. The whole ordeal—my father's assault, living in fear of further retribution, and the numerous sexual assaults he endured—sent him over the edge; he was eventually transferred to Napa State Hospital, a mental institution in northern California.

Not surprisingly, my parents split up following the episode with Rex. My mom took me, Chris, Autumn and Jason, who was just a few weeks old at the time, to Antioch, about five miles from Oakley. It wasn't long before she shacked up with another biker named Indian Larry. Meanwhile, my dad continued to live in the area, but we saw him only once in a while in the months before Mom took us to South Dakota, where things got even worse.

SOMETIME IN 1981 my mother left Indian Larry and decided we would be better off a long way from the Pittsburg-Antioch-Oakley area. Chris and I didn't want to leave and be separated from Dad, but since he was 10 and I was eight our opinions didn't matter. Like me, my older brother both feared and worshiped our dad, even though he wasn't even Chris' biological father (a fact our mother didn't share with us until about five years later). Despite our protests we headed to Rapid City, South Dakota, where my mom's sister, Lori, lived. After we left, my dad's separation from his kids sank him further into despair and, I later learned, deeper into the underworld of drug use and trafficking.

Anxious to get out of California, my mom sold most of our belongings, put what we kept in cardboard boxes, and carted the boxes and her four kids onto a Greyhound to Rapid City. After a couple of weeks with my Aunt Lori, my mom got a job as a barmaid in the town of Custer, about 30 miles south of Rapid City.

Mom got an apartment in Custer with Chris, Autumn and Jason in tow. But we didn't have much room, so I ended up living on a small ranch outside of Custer for about a year with a couple, Gary and Toots Worth, who were friends of my parents.

I also skipped the fourth grade that year.

Having moved from one state to another, then to a different residence than the rest my family, I somehow fell through the cracks of the South Dakota educational system and wasn't registered with the local school district. My mom never placed much value on our education and didn't care if I went to school or not. So I spent the 1981-82 school year working as a ranch hand for Gary and Toots—riding tractors that summer and fall, milking cows, feeding animals, fixing fences and barns, making butter, and even decapitating chickens, which I hated. All in all, it was the most idyllic time of my young life and a wonderful change from the dysfunctional environment I was used to.

Unfortunately, my reprieve from my mother's bad decisions came to an end in 1982 when she moved all of us back to Rapid City after she met a man and decided to move in with him. It was a huge mistake. In her late 20s at the time, my mom was very attractive and had no problem meeting men; but most of the guys with whom she became involved were mean, abusive lowlifes, and the guy she shacked up with in Rapid City (I'll call him Brent) was as mean and abusive as they came.

My mother and Brent met in the bar in which she worked. He was a well-built, good-looking guy with rugged features, the kind my mother seemed to attract, and it wasn't long before she quit her job in Custer and moved in with him in a two-story rental, bringing her four kids with her. Jason was only two years old at the time and didn't know any better, but Chris, Autumn and I quickly grew to hate Brent—especially Chris. Brent was a construction worker, a martial arts enthusiast, a rodeo cowboy—and one mean asshole. Years later when I watched the movie *Urban Cowboy*, the evil and abusive character, Wes, played by Scott Glenn, brought bitter and disturbing memories of Brent to mind.

Our mother left California to seek a better life for herself and her kids, but when she decided to live with Brent, she instead dragged us into a nightmare of constant dread and recurring physical abuse. My mother's relationship with Brent wasn't much different than the ones she had with our dad and the other men she met: They drank excessively, did drugs regularly, and fought incessantly. Unlike our father, who despite his many faults did not abuse his kids, Brent made our time with him a living hell. My siblings and I lived in constant terror when we were around him, speaking only when necessary for fear of getting slapped across the face or knocked to the ground for saying something he didn't like.

I was nine, a shy, passive kid at the time, kind of pudgy and an easy target for Brent's sadistic tendencies. When Brent would hit or slap me, which was often, I would cry and beg him to stop, unable to defend myself. Chris, on the other hand, used a different approach to cope with Brent's cruelty. He was a stoic kid who kept his hatred for Brent bottled up inside. When Brent would hit Chris, he would glare at him and through the tears say something like, "Are you finished?" But I could tell Brent's constant abuse was taking its toll on him.

One night, after we had endured Brent's brutality for more than a year, Chris decided he had had enough. It started a day or two earlier when Brent came home and found Autumn, who was six or seven, and Jason playing in the bathtub. Brent was drunk or stoned or both, and when he walked into the bathroom he went ballistic because of the water Autumn and Jason had splashed onto the floor. He pulled both kids out of the tub and beat their naked little bodies viciously and unmercifully. I can still hear my little sister and brother screaming for help. But Chris and I were powerless to do anything. It still makes me ill to think about it.

A few nights later Chris saw his chance. As they did many evenings, Mom and Brent got high and did some serious partying. By 2 a.m. they were both passed out, Mom on a couch in the living room on the main floor and Brent in their bedroom on the second level. Chris and I were in our beds in the room we shared in the basement when Chris announced his plan.

"Joe," he whispered, "I'm gonna kill Brent tonight."

It wasn't the first time my brother had uttered these words, but this time he sounded dead serious.

"What?!" I replied.

"He's passed out," Chris said. "This is my chance. I'm gonna kill him. I can't take it anymore."

"How?"

"With these."

From under his bed, Chris pulled out a couple of bricks he found in a nearby field. I was shocked, afraid to say anything.

We both lay in our beds in silence. I could hear Chris breathing hard. I knew he was scared to death and trying to work up the courage to follow through with his plan.

After what seemed like an eternity, Chris spoke again. "Joe, you need to come with me."

But I shook my head, frozen in fear.

"Fine," Chris said. "I'll do it myself."

Sitting on the edge of his bed, Chris removed his pillow from its pillowcase, carefully placed the bricks in the pillowcase, took a deep breath, put his feet on the floor, walked out of the room and slowly up the basement stairs, into the living room, and past our sleeping mother. I trailed after my brother up the basement stairs; I could see his body shaking in fear. I cautiously walked into the living room but was afraid to go any farther. I watched from the bottom of the stairs as Chris went up to the second floor. I heard his footsteps as he walked down the hallway toward the bedroom where Brent was in a deep sleep. My heart was pounding so loudly I thought it would wake up my mother. I was never so scared in my life. Suddenly, Brent let out a blood-curdling scream from the floor above.

Chris came racing down the stairs in a panic and flew out the front door. Knowing I would be accused of being my brother's accomplice, I quickly followed Chris out the door.

With his head and face bleeding profusely, Brent staggered down the stairs screaming and swearing. Briefly confused, our mother got up from the living room couch; when she saw us bolt out of the house she knew right away it was Chris who had attacked Brent. Lucky for us she managed to convince Brent that his assailant was an intruder, which didn't take much convincing given the shape Brent was in and the number of enemies he had. Fortunately, Brent was in no condition to do much more than wipe the blood from his face, climb up the stairs, and collapse back into bed.

Scared out of our wits, Chris and I stayed away from the apartment the next day, not that Brent noticed; he spent that day and evening sleeping off his bender and the injuries from Chris' attack. When we called Mom, she told us Brent still didn't know who had attacked him, but if we stayed away any longer, he might get suspicious. So with much trepidation we returned to the apartment the next evening. Brent had a huge black eye and the rest of his face was a mess, but he said he was well enough to go to work the next day. Chris had given it his best shot but he was only 11 and was neither big enough nor strong enough to inflict the kind of damage he was going for.

Chris and I were still very frightened. We knew if Brent even *thought* we were responsible for his injuries, we were in for horrific beatings, or worse. Our mom had the same fear. "What the hell were you thinking?!" she hissed at Chris when Brent was out of earshot. "He'll kill you if he finds out! He'll kill all of us!"

Our mother's frightful prediction was no exaggeration. Given Brent's violent nature, she knew we were *all* in serious danger. Brent was a human volcano ready to explode, and we all knew his fury could be lethal. "This whole situation is wrong," Mom said. "We need to get out of here."

The next morning Mom made Brent's lunch, kissed him goodbye, and watched him walk out the door, get in his car, and head to work. As soon as his car was out of sight she gave Chris and me two boxes each. "You boys pack whatever you can in these," she said. "We've got to get out of here now; we've got eight hours before Brent gets back."

She called her sister. "The kids and I need to leave town because I think Brent might kill us," she told Aunt Lori. "I can't stay with you because your place will be the first place he looks."

We left most of our belongings and all of our furniture in the apartment; Mom even left her motorcycle behind—a vintage 1950 Harley-Davidson Panhead. Running for our lives, we went to a shelter for battered women. When Brent returned to an empty house later that day and contacted Lori, she told him she didn't know where we were. A day or so later when Mom was certain Brent was at work, we boarded a bus for Medford, Oregon, where Mom had a few friends and relatives.

Knowing we were headed back to the West Coast, Chris and I begged to see our dad. I don't know how much our mom told our dad about Brent, but when they talked on the phone, my parents agreed it would be a good idea for Dad to take Chris and me for a while. Still living in Pittsburg, Dad decided he wanted to earn a better wage and was attending trade school to become an electrician. When we arrived at the bus depot in Medford, Dad and a buddy of his, Walter Parsons, were waiting for us. Chris and I were overjoyed. Mom and Dad made our little family reunion in the bus station brief. Chris and I kissed our mother and our little brother and sister goodbye, put our boxes in Walter's van, and headed for California. We had escaped Brent's wrath, and that was certainly a good thing. But just as certain, living with Dad would prove to be anything but peaceful or normal.

WHEN CHRIS AND I first arrived at our new home we were shocked. Pittsburg has more than its share of bad neighborhoods, and 555 W. 10th Street, No. 7 was in the middle of what can only be described as a ghetto. Dad's residence was a part of the ratty, ramshackle Pittsburg housing projects—a small, unkempt place with a single bedroom. The streets were infested with crime, and the storefronts were dilapidated hangouts for drug addicts and prostitutes. As far as I could tell, Dad, Chris and I were the only white people within several blocks. The immediate area was predominantly black with some Asians and Hispanics. Given our dad's intolerance and bigotry, it seemed odd (and somewhat ironic) to be living in a neighborhood where *we* were the minority.

Chris and I did our best to keep a low profile and steer clear of dangerous areas. But as two of only a few white kids in the vicinity, there were times when we were the object of threats and racial taunts, especially from the drunks and crack addicts who loitered in front of "Pete's Liquor," two blocks down 10th Street and the only store within walking distance of our apartment. Dad would often send Chris and me to Pete's for milk, a loaf of bread, or other food.

For as long as I live, my older brother will always be one of the bravest people I know because of how, as an 11-year-old, he tried to protect us from Brent, who, we later learned from our mother, was shot and killed in a bar fight in South Dakota. But when it came to living among the crackheads, criminals and gang members in our neighborhood, he couldn't cope. After about six months in Pittsburg, he called our mom. "Come and get me," he said. "I can't take it."

Mom didn't have a car, so she hitchhiked the 300 miles from Medford to Pittsburg. When she arrived at our apartment, Dad was at work. She grabbed me by the shoulder and said, "You're coming, too."

I was only 10, but this time I adamantly refused to cooperate. Given my mother's history of hooking up with violent men like Brent, not to mention the other vagaries of her lifestyle, I wasn't about to possibly live that nightmare again. "I'm not going and you can't make me!" I screamed. After a few minutes of arguing, she realized I wasn't going to budge. And without a vehicle, she wasn't in a position to remove me from the apartment against my will. "OK, Joe, have it your way," she said with a shrug. "Your brother and I are leaving right now. If that's the way you want it, it's your funeral." And with that, she and Chris left.

From that day until my dad died six years later, it was just my father and me living together in the slums of Pittsburg.

IT WASN'T THE best of living conditions, but it was as stable a household as anything I had known. It was also nice to have other family nearby; my dad's brother and his future wife, my Uncle Gary and Aunt Dina, and my paternal grandmother, Minda O'Brien, all lived in Pittsburg. Nevertheless, it wasn't long after Chris left that I began to have second thoughts about my decision to stay with my dad.

My father did not flaunt his drug habits in front of me, but he didn't really hide them either. Nor did he disguise his disdain for the leaders and politicians who took a dim view of illegal drug use. One evening we were watching TV together when then-President Ronald Reagan and his wife, Nancy, appeared on the screen. As part of the Reagan administration's War on Drugs, the president and first lady were featured in an ad touting Mrs. Reagan's "Just Say No" campaign. I made the mistake of asking Dad what he thought of their message.

"Fuck 'em!" he spat. "Fuck 'em all! They're just rich, asshole politicians! They don't struggle to make a living! They don't live in a slum! What the fuck do they know?!"

"Ohh-kaay," I said under my breath, regretting that I had broached the subject.

A few months later Dad returned home from one of his three-day benders and promptly crashed on the living room couch, falling asleep for several hours before waking up with an empty stomach. "Joe," he said, "go to Pete's and get me a Snickers bar and a Coke, and get some milk if we need it." Then he went back to sleep.

I usually made such transactions at Pete's with my own change. When I arrived at the store, the dozen or so drug addicts, panhandlers and other shady characters were standing or sitting on the sidewalk out front, as usual. One of them started hassling me as I tried to enter the store. "Hey, boy, give me your money," he barked. When I balked, he pushed me to the ground and threatened to get even more violent. I scurried home crying and told my dad what had happened. Hung-over and hungry, he was in no mood for my sob story and sent me back to Pete's.

I returned to the store with my coins in my fist, hoping to avoid another confrontation. But the same guy, a belligerent, strung-out black man in his 30s, again demanded my money. When I tried to get past him and enter the store, he hit my hand and sent the change flying onto the sidewalk. He and some of the other men scrambled after the coins; I raced home again, blubbering all the way. When I woke Dad to tell him I still didn't have his Coke and candy bar, he angrily told me to return to Pete's and not to come back without them.

"Dad," I cried, "I'm not going back there! Those guys in front of the store are messing with me! One of them hit my arm and I lost all my change!"

But he wasn't interested in my predicament. "Get your ass up there, goddamn it!" he yelled. "Do what the fuck I tell you!"

"Dad," I implored, "I can't do it! I'm only 11, and they're a bunch of grown-ups!"

"I DON'T GIVE A SHIT!" my father replied at the top of his voice. "DO WHAT I TELL YOU!"

I was screwed—stuck between my father's unreasonable command and the threats of the addicts in front of Pete's. Scared stiff, I reluctantly gathered some more change from my stash of coins and returned to Pete's for the third time. But I lost my nerve when I saw the man who roughed me up and the others still loitering in front of the store.

When I returned, Dad was asleep, but he heard me enter the apartment. "Joe, where's the Coke and the Snickers bar?" he asked.

In between sobs I gave him the answer I knew would set him off: "I don't have them. I couldn't buy them. I told you, they pushed me down and popped my hand and took my money. And when I went back, they were still there." I started crying again.

After three days of partying and in need of sustenance, Dad was in no mood for my excuses; as I feared, he went ballistic. As he got up from the couch, I knew somebody was going to pay. All he was wearing was a pair of jeans. His eyes were red and his hair was a mess. "This is bullshit!" he said. He grabbed me, seized his .38 Special off the floor, dragged me out of the house, and threw me in his car. He raced the two blocks down 10th Street to Pete's and screeched to a halt in front of the store. My tormentor and the others were still there.

He yanked me out of the car, pulled out his gun from his jeans, pointed it at the group of men, looked at me and yelled, "Which one of these fuckin' niggers was hassling you?! Pick him out and I'll shoot the motherfucker! Do you see him?!"

The men scattered. Shirtless, shoeless and with a crazed look in his eyes, Dad shot two rounds in the air and yelled, "If any of you fuck with my son again, I'll fuckin' kill you!" Dad grabbed me, dragged me back into the car, drove back home, still without his Coke and Snickers, and five minutes later he was back on the couch, sound asleep.

An hour or so later, the police came knocking at our door. "Dad … Dad … the cops are here," I said, shaking like a leaf.

He looked up at me from the couch. "I don't give a fuck," he replied with complete disinterest.

Bang, bang, bang.

"Dad, don't you think we better answer the door?" I asked.

Finally, he got up and answered the door; two uniformed policemen stood outside. "Did you just have a deal go down at Pete's?" one of them asked.

"I don't know what the fuck you're talking about," Dad said.

"We heard you shot a gun," the cop said.

"I said I don't know what you're talking about. Are you gonna arrest me? Because if you're not, I'm busy." After a few more questions, the officers left, and Dad went back to bed.

The episode in front of Pete's Liquor wasn't the only time my dad resorted to gunplay to express his displeasure. A year or so later, an acquaintance of my father's offered to install a transmission in a 1956 Ford Dad had rebuilt. The guy's fee was some of the methamphetamine to which my dad had plenty of access. But the guy must have been using some of his payment while he was doing the job because he royally screwed up the installment, which severely damaged the Ford. My dad tried to contact the guy about making reparations, but he never returned my father's calls. Big mistake. A few months later, the guy was visiting someone in the neighborhood and parked his car down the street from where we lived. When Dad saw the guy's vehicle, he got his gun and strolled down the street to the parked car. Then, in broad daylight, he unloaded an entire clip into the car's hood and grill. He then walked back to our apartment as if nothing happened.

That's when I started to call my dad "Crazy Pops."

CHAPTER
2

THE TATTOO ON MY RIGHT BICEPS reads "In Memory of Dad"; I got it in the spring of my senior year of high school, a few months after he died of a heroin overdose. The image includes a Harley-Davidson Shovelhead engine and a rising sun. "Shovelhead at dawn," Dad used to say, referring to his early-morning motorcycle rides over the highways and back roads of northern California following one of his drug- and/or alcohol-induced escapades.

Those trips were sometimes dangerous and often involved illegal activity, but he didn't need to venture far from Pittsburg to tempt fate. Partying one night at a Pittsburg bowling alley frequented by bikers, Dad and some of his group decided to continue their revelry at a bar in Antioch, five miles east on Highway 4. They left the bowling alley on their choppers around midnight, drove onto the Highway 4 eastbound ramp, and headed to Antioch. But my father, undoubtedly under the influence, decided to add a little excitement to his excursion. He drove past the entrance ramp, over the overpass and took a right, intentionally going the wrong way onto the exit ramp coming off westbound Highway 4. He proceeded to drive to

Antioch *going 100 mph against oncoming traffic for five miles*, meeting his astounded friends a few minutes later at the next bar.

Fortunately, my father's self-destructive tendencies were mitigated by his interest and involvement in my athletic endeavors. He was an outstanding athlete in his day and was going to make damn sure I followed in his footsteps—even if he had to bend the rules to get me into the local Junior Football League a year early.

Boys entering California's JFL programs for the first time had to be 11 years old at the start of the season. When I started the sixth grade in September 1983, I was two months shy of my 11th birthday and therefore ineligible to play football that fall, which was fine with me. I was a big kid, but I was more chunky than hunky and didn't particularly care for football's inherent violence. But Dad somehow doctored my paperwork or birth certificate or convinced somebody to let me play; I don't know how he did it, but within a few days I found myself decked out in football gear and playing for the 49ers of the Pittsburg JFL for 11-year-olds.

But I was far from thrilled. In fact, I was perfectly content to stick to baseball where I was almost always the biggest and strongest kid on the diamond, a Little League and Pony League all-star catcher and hard-throwing relief pitcher who intimidated the opposition. But at the same time I was self-conscious about my ample girth, a little quiet, and even shy. I remember more than once the taunts from people in the stands when I took the mound as a Little Leaguer. "Hey, there's the O'Brien kid! Check his ID!" they would yell. "Hey, O'Brien, you need a shave! Hey, O'Brien, who do you work for, the [local] steel mill?"

Despite my athletic ability and heft, I did nothing out of the ordinary during the 49ers' preseason practices to make my coaches notice me, and I was relegated to the kickoff and kick return teams as we prepared for our season opener. As one of the biggest players on my team (though the youngest), I was afraid I might be the target of fans' jeers on the gridiron like I had been on the diamond. But it never happened. In fact, my perspective changed entirely on the first play of my first game in organized football.

The game was played in Pittsburg High's stadium with my dad and his brother, Gary, in the stands. On kickoffs I was assigned as a "wedge buster," a player who lines up next to the kicker, runs down the middle of the field, and collides with the blockers on the other team to break up the wedge protecting the kick returner. I was extremely nervous as I took my position for the opening kickoff. As the ball was booted to the opposing team, I felt a sudden rush—an electrifying combination of fearlessness and exhilaration—I threw my head back, extended my arms and started to scream "Aaaaahhhhhhh!" as I raced down the field. My dad heard me all the way up in the stands and later said he at first thought I had pulled a muscle or somehow hurt myself because he never heard me yell like that.

As the two teams converged, I hit the first opposing player I saw. I caught him going full speed and every law of physics seemed to work in my favor at that moment: I rammed my shoulder pads into his sternum, raised my helmet under his facemask, lifted him off the ground, and drove him into the turf. He let out a groan as I quickly got to my feet. As I stood over my vanquished opponent, caught up in the moment of that hit and amazed by the punishment I had just delivered, I let go with an intensely satisfying sound of my own from the depths of my lungs: "*Whooooaa!*" I also remember my dad up in the stands shouting his approval.

And I was hooked.

In my excitement, I failed to notice that the other team had returned the kickoff for a touchdown, but at the moment I didn't even care. The ecstasy I derived from that single hit was the highest high I had ever experienced. At that instant, on that one play, everything changed: I knew I was born to play football.

I'm no psychologist, but I think my football epiphany that day was the discovery of a way to give vent to the cruelties I had endured and the abuse and violence I had witnessed as a child. Almost overnight, I underwent a transformation: I was no longer that bashful, pudgy white kid, but someone to reckon with in the hallways of my school and on the streets of my neighborhood. As if someone had suddenly thrown a switch in my brain, football gave me a sense of purpose and an emotional outlet where I could make the most of my athletic skills, channel my aggression, and impose my will on others with impunity. I felt indomitable, and that feeling was sublime. From that point I approached football not as a pastime or a hobby, but as a way of life. And at every level—from JFL ball in the sixth and seventh grades, to Pop Warner ball in the eighth grade, to high school, college and the pros—I played the game all out and the way it is supposed to be played: physically, viciously and aggressively.

As a sixth-grader, I went from a quiet, overweight kid to a football standout and the toughest 11-year-old on the face of the earth (or so I thought). As a seventh- and eighth-grader in Pittsburg's Central Junior High I wasn't a bully (I hate bullies) or a troublemaker, but I developed an attitude that led to a reputation as someone people didn't mess with. However, given the demographics of my school, that reputation didn't come without its issues. As a white student who was also a bruiser within a predominantly African-American student body, I was involved in a few altercations that were racially motivated. Despite the influence of my father's racial intolerance, I always did my best to judge my fellow students—and all people, for that matter—by their character and not their color. But if provoked, I was more than willing to settle things after school with a few black classmates who thought I needed to be put in my place.

As a junior high student my infatuation with football and all the positive things it embodies—competition, hard work, intelligence, determination, character, teamwork, dedication, mental and physical toughness—marked the beginning of my lifelong love affair with the game. Ironically, it was around the same time that I began my protracted (and secret) relationship with drugs. My initial foray into what would later become heavy use of methamphetamine and GHB began as typical youthful indiscretion with beer and marijuana when I was 11. When my dad would take off on his Harley to go on one of his benders and leave me unsupervised for a day or two, I would drink some of the beer in our refrigerator if I was certain he wouldn't notice a few missing bottles or cans. I first tried marijuana when I was in the seventh grade as I was walking to school one morning with a friend. He pulled out a joint, informed me that he occasionally smoked weed before class, and invited me to join him. I didn't really want to partake, but I also didn't want to seem uncool, so I took a couple of hits. It was not an enjoyable experience; I was paranoid about being caught and unable to concentrate on my studies the entire morning.

Those initial experiments were not part of my regular routine. For the most part I maintained my focus on the gridiron, and after two seasons of JFL ball I moved up to Pop Warner football, which recognizes both athletic and academic excellence, and played on the line for the Nomads of the West Pittsburg Youth Football Association. But first I had to drop about 10 pounds to get to the 135-pound weight limit for 12-year-olds. Pop Warner ball was a significant step up in the level of competition and intensity, and teams actually traveled to other cities to play. We competed against opponents from Pleasant Hill, Moraga, Concord and other nearby cities, and I continued to use my size, skill and unbridled ferocity to enhance my reputation as one of the area's dominant players. I was also a good student when I put my mind to it, and as an eighth-grader at Central I pulled a 4.0 grade point average for the entire year.

My combined athletic and academic performances that fall led to my first major award: I was named the area's top Pop Warner player. A few weeks later I received the ultimate honor for those playing youth football: I was chosen as one of 35 first-team eighth-grade Pop Warner Scholar All-Americans for 1985, which is quite impressive when you consider there were about 350,000 Pop Warner participants nationwide at the time. I flew to Philadelphia with my Aunt Dina for the national awards ceremony and received my All-America certificate from sportscaster and former coach Dick Vermeil and Eagles quarterback Ron Jaworski. But it was a bittersweet experience because my dad was unable to attend the event. He was in prison at the time.

IN MARCH 1985, around 3 a.m. on a Friday when I was in the seventh grade, my father rushed into my bedroom in a state of panic. Like he did many nights, he had been at a bar, leaving me home alone, and was quite inebriated. I could tell right away something was seriously wrong; there was a fear in his voice, a fear I had never heard before.

"Joe! Joe! Wake up!" he said with great urgency. "I need your help! I hit somebody with my car! I think it was a woman and I think I killed her."

"What?!" I said as I sat upright in my bed.

"Yeah," he snapped, "I need you to wash the car."

"Right now?"

"Yeah, RIGHT NOW!"

Even though it was the middle of the night, I wasn't going to argue with him. Grabbing a flashlight, I went outside to examine Dad's 1973 Cadillac Coupe de Ville and saw why he wanted me to wash it: Embedded in a large dent in the front fender on the passenger side were fresh blood and what looked like chunks of human flesh.

After a night of partying in Concord, Dad was returning to Pittsburg with a friend. He was speeding and driving recklessly, passing slower vehicles on both the left and right. While he was passing a vehicle on a Willow Pass Road entrance ramp to Highway 4 at the Willow Pass Grade he accidentally struck 36-year-old Sandra Jablonski of Antioch who was standing on the roadside beside her car after it broke down. After he hit the woman and her car, Dad panicked and kept driving—a classic case of hit-and-run. When he dropped his friend off, Dad threatened him with great bodily harm, or worse, if he reported the accident.

I got a hose and did my best to wash off the "evidence" stuck on Dad's Cadillac; when I finished he got in the car and drove off. Several hours later he returned home. "Where's the car?" I asked.

"I got rid of it," he said. "Just keep your mouth shut. If anyone asks where the car is or where I was last night, just tell them you don't know."

But Dad's cover-up was seriously flawed. His passenger's conscience got to him, and the friend called the police a day or so later and told them about the accident. When the cops showed up, Dad denied everything, but the evidence against him piled up quickly. Some neighbors told the police they saw me washing the Cadillac the night of the fatality, and a forensic pathologist, using DNA evidence, found some of the victim's blood on the ground where I had washed the car. About a week later the California Highway Patrol found my dad's abandoned car near Oakley. "Investigators, acting on an informant's tip, arrested Scott O'Brien at his Pittsburg home," the Antioch *Daily Ledger* reported in early April. "O'Brien, who has a record of convictions for drunk and reckless driving, was arrested on suspicion of felony hit-and-run in connection with the death of Sandra Jablonski." Dad was convicted of vehicular manslaughter and sentenced to three years in prison, eventually serving 18 months.

It was a terrible, gut-wrenching ordeal. I was filled with sadness for the victim and her family and humiliated by my father's arrest and conviction. Once again, life had gone horribly awry because of a bad decision by one of my parents. Fortunately, I had a support system in Pittsburg with my grandmother and Uncle Gary and Aunt Dina, who were named my guardians during my dad's incarceration. Gary and Dina lived directly across the street from my grandmother, which made it convenient for me to stay at both places.

IN THE FALL of 1986, soon after the start of my freshman year at Pittsburg High, my father was released from prison. My Uncle Gary and Aunt Dina, who later divorced, were generous and caring surrogate parents in my dad's absence, but I was an impressionable 13-year-old who still idolized my father despite all the pain and suffering he had caused, and I happily returned to his custody when he got out. But there was something different about him: He was meaner and more unreasonable than ever, and his obsession with my football career became downright absurd— so much so that for all intents and purposes he sentenced me to my own personal prison the following summer.

At the end of my first semester of high school I got four A's and two B's for my final grades, which I thought were perfectly acceptable. But to my surprise, Dad was not pleased. "This is bullshit," he said as he reviewed my report card. "If you're going to play big-time college football, you're going to have to do better than this. I'm telling you right now, if you don't exceed these grades next semester, or match them at the very least, you're going to be grounded for the summer."

I learned long ago that it was unwise to argue with my father. So I figured I would just make sure I continued to get acceptable grades and avoid any problems. However, an unfortunate set of circumstances the following semester led to my summer from hell. First, Dad and I lived a couple of miles from Pittsburg High, which meant I needed a ride from him to school each morning. Second, that spring I was scheduled to take driver's education, which began at 7 a.m., an hour before regular classes started. Third, because California state law required specific amounts of training and driving hours, punctuality and attendance were factors in each student's final grade. Fourth, given my father's proclivity for partying on an almost nightly basis, my prompt arrival at 7 most mornings was dubious at best. Fifth, and most damning, driver's ed grades were part of each student's report card.

When I got my grades at the end of the spring semester, I again pulled four A's and two B's, but I got a C in driver's ed because of my frequent tardiness. When he saw my report card, Dad went ballistic. "What is this shit?!" he yelled. "A fuckin' C?! Are you kidding me?! I warned you, Joe. You're on restriction from now until you start football practice."

I was incredulous. "What?! But it's *driver's ed*. It's not even a real class! Besides, that C is because you made me late for class a bunch of times! This isn't fair!"

"Don't argue with me, goddamn it!" he said. "If you knew you were gonna be late, then you should have fuckin' walked to school."

Grounded until August and fearing I would make matters even worse if I pressed the issue, I stomped out of the room. My hope was that he would eventually realize how preposterous his reasoning was and soften his stance. I should have known better; he wasn't the type to change his mind. Of all the grief he had caused me, this decision had to be the most infuriating and ironic of them all: He demanded so much of me while he himself led a life that was rife with violence, substance abuse, dangerous behavior, and other criminal activity.

But none of that mattered. True to his word, Dad restricted me to our small house in inner city Pittsburg the entire summer between my freshman and sophomore years; I couldn't even use the phone. I guess he thought he was instilling in me the discipline I sorely lacked while he was out drinking, doing drugs, and getting into bar fights. I also quickly learned he was not kidding about turning me into a "serious" football player during my three-month confinement.

In early June he purchased a set of weights and set them up in our basement—The Dungeon I called it because of the torment I endured there. "You need to bulk up if you're going to be the kind of player I expect you to be," he said. "You're going to lift every day this summer. Then be ready for roadwork when I get home from work."

For the next 12 weeks I spent countless hours lifting those wretched weights. Each day was filled with intense pain and sheer drudgery as I pushed myself—screaming in frustration and anger at the loneliness, unfairness and injustice of it all. But my training regimen didn't end with my daily lifting. On the first Monday of my summer "vacation," Dad pulled up in front of our house in his 1956 Chevy pickup and revved its 327 engine. That became my signal to quickly get out of the house and join him in the truck. "OK, it's time for you to get your ass in shape," he announced. A 12-pack of beer was at his side.

We drove about seven or eight miles out of Pittsburg. Dad stopped the truck on a rural road in the middle of nowhere. The temperature was in the 80s. "OK, get out and start running," he ordered.

At first, I wasn't sure what was going on. "But where?" I asked. "Where am I going?"

"Start running toward town," he replied. "I'm gonna drive ahead and finish my beer. You'll know you're done when you see the pickup."

I reluctantly got out and stood by the side of the road as my dad drove off. "Jesus Christ, you've got to be kidding," I muttered as the Chevy disappeared in the distance.

Each Monday through Friday around 5 p.m. for the rest of the summer, Dad would pull up to the house in his pickup and gun the engine. The first thing I did when I got in the truck was look and see if he had a six- or a 12-pack. The former usually meant I was in for about a four- or five-mile run; the latter usually meant seven or so miles.

But my daily ordeal didn't always end with those evening runs. Two or three times a week when we got home, Dad, despite his intake of beer, would decide that we needed to lift together in The Dungeon. He was an experienced weightlifter, and although he wasn't always in the best of cardiovascular shape (his weight fluctuated anywhere between

250 to 300 pounds), he was always very strong. That was one reason I was afraid to disobey my father. He never struck me, but he didn't have to because I did everything I was told to do out of fear.

In less than a month my strength and endurance increased noticeably. Given my progress and the fact I complied with my dad's wishes with little complaint, I thought he might relax the restrictions he had imposed, but he never did. So I ran and I lifted, and I lifted and I ran. And I lifted some more. In late June, I worked up the courage to ask my father for a one-day furlough two months down the road. "Dad, I really want to go to the county fair in August with this girl," I said. "Can I go if I bench-press a certain amount?"

He seemed amused. "OK," he said, "we can make a deal. What did you start benching at?"

"Around 200," I replied.

"What do you think you can bench by the end of August?"

"Well, I think I'll be able to do 275 pounds by then."

He laughed. "Get serious. There's no way you're going to bench that much by then. Sure, if you can bench 275 pounds when the fair comes around, I'll let you go."

That's all the incentive I needed. Less than a month later after one of my evening runs, I made an announcement: "Dad, you need to come downstairs. I've got something to show you." And I benched 275 pounds. A couple of weeks later I benched 295 pounds. By mid-August I reached 300 pounds. A few days before the fair I benched 315 pounds—40 pounds more than our agreed-upon target weight.

Throughout the time I tortured myself to reach my goal, I assumed my reprieve to attend the fair would be a daylong outing. On the morning I was to receive my reward and enjoy a few hours of freedom, I said to my dad, "OK, my friend John is going to pick me up at 11:30. We're going to meet this girl I like and some other friends. I'll be home by 11 p.m."

But my father had other plans: "You ain't going at 11:30," he replied. "You're leaving at 8 p.m., and you'll be back by 10. And you better not be late."

I was stunned and furious. But as usual, I held my anger inside; there was no point in trying to reason with him. I called my friend who picked me up at 8 that evening. I was so afraid of losing track of time, I was home by 9:30.

I WAS NEVER so glad for a school year to begin as I was that fall. With the start of classes and my sophomore season of football, I was finally free from my father's unreasonable restrictions and his overzealous plans to make me a football star before I was 15. But I must admit, due at least in part to my arduous workouts that summer, I felt pretty good about the change in my physical appearance. My body had transformed from stocky to powerful, and the change in my physique greatly improved my self-esteem.

Thanks in large part to my Aunt Dina, I also became an active member of Pitt High's student body and assumed a variety of leadership roles. It was Dina who recognized my communications and leadership skills while I was an underclassman and encouraged me to use that talent to my advantage beyond the football field and locker room. A volleyball and basketball standout and student body president when she herself was a student at Pittsburg High, she urged me to get involved in student government and run for office. "Look, you're a natural-born leader," she said. "You're the captain of every team you play on. People look up to you. If you want to become a bona fide football prospect to a college, you need to have more than a pile of football awards. You need to be involved in extracurricular activities to show them you're a well-rounded student-athlete and not just another jock."

It was some of the best advice I ever received. Dina's guidance helped me come out of my shell and allowed me to develop leadership skills I didn't know I had. I began to flourish at Pitt High, not only as a standout athlete and a good student, but also as a leader among the school's racially mixed student body. In fact, I took my aunt's advice and ran for sophomore class president. And to my amazement, I won.

As the 1987-88 academic year began it seemed I was coming into my own; even though I was just 14 I already believed I was destined to do great things. Football stardom, scholarship offers, a college education, and other accomplishments were in the offing and all just a matter of time. I felt my potential was unlimited, and so did many of my peers and superiors. As sophomore class president and captain of the junior varsity football team, I enjoyed the respect and admiration of not only my fellow students, but also the teachers, coaches and administrators at PHS.

Unfortunately, beneath that veneer of propriety and virtue came the emergence of an alter ego, a second side to my personality that was pulling me in the opposite direction of the greatness and success that so many thought were my destiny. As a sophomore I became a methamphetamine user.

CHAPTER
3

THE FIRST TIME I TRIED METH was at a bonfire involving dozens of teenagers along the San Joaquin River. Most of the revelers that Friday night were Pittsburg High upperclassmen, but as a popular, well-known jock, I was considered one of the cool kids and got invited to join the "party." One bad choice doesn't usually change a person's life, but my decision that night was a horrendous mistake that would eventually lead me on a perilous journey of dishonesty and deceit—more than 15 years of leading a double life.

Strangely enough, after returning home from the bonfire that night I ended up spending the next few hours with my father, who, ironically, was also high on meth—although neither of us ever admitted it to the other.

I arrived home just before my 11 p.m. curfew. I was pretty amped up and knew I had to quickly try to straighten up and appear sober because I knew my dad was up late studying for his journeyman electrician's license. As I entered the house Dad was sitting at our living room table with an open textbook and a yellow note pad in front of him. I could tell right away he had done some meth. Although my father didn't openly take narcotics in front of me, his in-home use was frequent. In fact, it became so common I could usually ascertain what drug he was on based on his mannerisms. On this particular night he told me he "took something" to help him concentrate, but I knew it was meth. Not in so many words, but my father had made it clear that his substance abuse didn't give me license to do the same, and with the summer from hell he put me through still fresh in my mind I was afraid I might suffer an even worse punishment if he realized I, too, was on drugs at that moment. The problem was I needed to walk past him to get to my bedroom. I figured my best bet was to utter a quick greeting without stopping, avoid eye contact, hope he wouldn't notice my altered state, and crawl into bed. Given Dad's own condition, I thought my chances were pretty good. I promised myself that if I could get by him undetected just this one time, I would never take meth again.

Trying to act and sound as normal as I could, I made my way to my bedroom. "G'night," I said. "I'm going to bed."

"Where you been?" Dad asked, without looking up from his book.

"At a party."

"Did you stay out of trouble?"

"Yeah."

"OK. G'night."

I got away with it! Or so I thought. But for the next two hours I stared at my bedroom ceiling as the methamphetamine coursed through my system. As I lay in my bed, the effects of the drug were typical of what I would later experience time and time again: euphoria, heightened alertness, and greater energy. My heartbeat and breathing increased, and the anxiety and fatigue I felt earlier dissipated. Despite my initial fear of getting caught and severely punished by my father, that no longer seem to matter; I had an increased sensation of self-confidence and ignored any semblance of common sense that said I should stay in my room, sleep off the effects of the meth, never tell my dad what I did, and never—ever—do it again. Instead, I got out of bed and walked into the living room, where my father was still studying.

"Dad, I can't sleep, can I help you with your homework?" I asked.

My offer wasn't that unusual. I would occasionally help him with his homework, asking him the sample questions in his books and manuals. But given the late hour, he raised his eyebrows and gave me a quizzical look.

"Did you take something tonight?" he asked.

"No," I replied. "Why do you ask?"

"Because it's 1 a.m. and you're telling me you can't sleep. You never 'can't sleep.'"

I tried not to act nonplussed. "I don't know what it is," I replied. "Hey, it's Friday night. There's no school tomorrow. I'm just not tired." I was starting to panic; for a frightening moment I thought I had really blown it, but to my utter surprise and immense relief, he decided not to continue his line of questioning. "OK," he said with a shrug. He pushed his book toward me. "There are some questions at the end of this chapter you can quiz me on."

In retrospect, I'm positive my dad knew I had taken some kind of drug, but given the circumstances, even *he* couldn't justify saying anything or punishing me when he himself was on meth. We stayed up until 4 a.m. working on his homework, and we never mentioned that episode again. When the time was right I always meant to ask my father about that night, but that time never came because two years later he was dead.

UNBEKNOWNST TO EVERYONE I knew—except those with whom I shared my illicit behavior—I continued to experiment with meth while I was in high school. My grade point average dipped to around 2.6 my sophomore year and I occasionally cut classes, but no one—not even my dad—seemed to notice. One reason I didn't raise any suspicions was because my athletic performance remained largely unaffected by my drug use. In fact, even though I increased my use of meth my junior and senior years, I put together a stellar three-sport career at Pittsburg High.

Of those three sports—baseball, wrestling and football—baseball came to me most naturally—due to the size, strength and athletic ability I inherited from both my parents. My four years with the Pirate baseball program were personally successful and gratifying; each year I was selected team captain and most inspirational player, and I was named MVP three times. I batted .416 as a sophomore on the junior varsity, and then hit .304 the following spring on the varsity under head coach Herc Pardi. As a senior I hit .375 and earned second-team All-Bay Valley Athletic League honors.

The varsity teams on which I played in 1989 and '90 didn't have enough pitching to be a legitimate contender in the BVAL, but we had a number of talented individuals. Outfielder Donny Sheppard was the Chicago White Sox's second-round pick in the 1989 amateur draft behind future major league star Frank Thomas of Auburn, while first baseman Jamie McLennan, shortstop Tommy Haase, and outfielder Benji Simonton all played college ball. I also had brief aspirations to play pro baseball when the Philadelphia Phillies expressed an interest in me as a catching prospect during my senior year. But their interest faded early in 1990 when I signed a letter of intent to play football at Santa Clara. Furthermore, by then I had developed the body of a football lineman, and at 245 pounds, I was, in the Phils' estimation, too big and bulky to be a big-league catcher. But I was OK with that; by then football had become my passion, and I knew it was my ticket to college and beyond.

While I had played baseball since I was five and football since I was 10, my interest in wrestling was more of an afterthought. I tried out for the PHS freshman basketball team and was the last player to make the cut. I was one of two white kids on the team and primarily did mop-up work in lopsided games. I wasn't very good and had more fouls than points at the end of the season. I concluded basketball wasn't for me and didn't play a winter sport my sophomore year.

In the middle of my junior year I decided to try out for the Pirate wrestling team because I thought it would be a good way to stay in shape for my senior year of football. But my dad didn't agree; he was concerned that I would have to lose weight to wrestle, and he wanted me to bulk up for football. I eventually convinced him that the benefits would outweigh the harm, and I started out the 1988-89 wrestling season on the junior varsity at 199 pounds. My options were to drop down to the 191-pound division or compete at heavyweight. The coaches thought it would be easy for me to lose eight pounds, but my father said absolutely not. He contacted head coach Brett McNamar: "If you make Joe lose one pound—if he comes home and starts spitting in a cup or starts running extra or I see him losing weight—I'm pulling him from the program," he said. "I'm telling you right now, he's gonna wrestle heavyweight or he's not gonna wrestle."

Turns out I was pretty good on the mat. After about two weeks on the JV I moved up to the varsity after I beat the varsity heavyweight. I went on to finish 22-9 in my combined JV and varsity matches that year, took second in the Bay Valley tournament, and fifth at the North Coast Sectional tournament. I was named the team MVP and most improved wrestler—pretty good for never having wrestled before. "Joe's always ready, the kind who always gets up for a match. He's definitely come a long way," McNamar told the *Pittsburg Post-Dispatch*, near the end of my junior season. "He's a super kid and a leader, too. He looks forward to competition. He doesn't run from it; he gets excited for it."

As a senior I was named team captain and wrestled at heavyweight between 235 and 245 pounds. During the regular season I went 35-3 as our team finished 6-1 in duals and took second in the BVAL. I took third in sectionals and won two out of my five matches in the California Interscholastic Federation state tournament, finishing seventh. At the end of the year I was again named the wrestling team's MVP.

BASEBALL WAS ENJOYABLE and wrestling helped make me disciplined and strong, but I was consumed by football. Throughout my career as a player and coach, the success of my team has always been vastly more important than any individual awards I was fortunate enough to receive. But it would be false modesty for me to ignore the fact I finished my high school career as one of the most honored football players to come out of Pitt. As a member of the freshman team, a sophomore on the junior varsity, and a junior on the Pirate varsity, I was named team captain, MVP and most inspirational player all three years. I played various positions on the line, but was primarily the center on offense and a tackle on defense. As a junior I earned second-team All-Bay Valley Athletic League honors at center as Pitt finished 5-5 overall and 4-3 in league play.

In the fall of 1989, my senior season, our team finished 6-4 overall and 5-2 in conference play under veteran coach Larry Rodriguez, good for second place in the BVAL. Given our failure to make the North Coast Sectional playoffs, it was a disappointing season from a team standpoint. But I thrived individually: I was named team captain, received more than 100 recruitment letters from some of the nation's top college football programs, was selected first-team All-BVAL at center and defensive tackle as well as first-team All-East Bay at center and honorable mention on defense. As a senior I racked up 77 tackles and 13 sacks; for my high school career I finished with 400 tackles and 54 sacks. "Joe was one of the better linemen we've had," Rodriguez told the *Post-Dispatch* after the '89 season. "[Because of] his attitude, his dedication to the game, his weight training, and being a team leader, players looked up to him." In May 2010, 20 years after I graduated from Pitt High, I was inducted into the school's Football Hall of Fame.

Although my devotion to the Pirate football program was authentic, the glowing example I supposedly set at PHS was misleading as my clandestine drug use continued. Even so, I continued to excel both on and off the field my senior year. At the start of the 1989-90 academic year I was elected as the student government's senior class representative, and I finished my final year with a 3.3 GPA. I also cleaned up when it came to individual awards. "Lineman Joe O'Brien needed help to take home the trophies he collected," said the *Post-Dispatch* in its coverage of the 46th annual Pittsburg Citizens Football Committee awards banquet. In addition to being named the Pirates' MVP and most inspirational player that fall, I was also named most outstanding lineman. Before the night was through I garnered two other honors: the George Lowry Memorial Award for season and off-season dedication and the Douglas Selby Vieira Memorial Award for citizenship and academic excellence. By the time I graduated from PHS the following spring, I received more than 70 athletic, academic and civic honors, including the Michael Becker Memorial Scholarship award, which goes to each graduating class' top student-athlete.

THE AWARDS AND accolades I received in high school were gratifying, but in the back of my mind I always felt guilty because of the drugs. But I never got caught. During the year and a half or so that I used meth before my father died, it was both easy and difficult to hide it from him: easy because he was gone so much, either working or partying; hard because the guilt was almost unbearable. By the end of my junior year meth was gaining control of my entire existence because it temporarily erased all my problems—all of the bad feelings and all the guilt that had accumulated during my life. I liked the rush and the escape it provided. Alcohol and marijuana became an afterthought; I didn't crave either and used them only when meth was not available.

Once I started using meth regularly, I fell in with a group of fellow users at school. But since I was a good student, a class officer, and captain of the football, baseball and wrestling teams, my friends went out of their way to keep my drug involvement under wraps. "If we're going to go out and get wasted tonight, we've got to protect Joe," one of them once said. "We can't let him get caught because he could lose his football scholarship."

I went right along with their scheme because I felt immense pressure to maintain my standing among my fellow students and the coaches and teachers at Pittsburg High—a position of esteem I had cultivated and others had chosen for me on the school's athletic fields and in its hallways and classrooms. I was a well-behaved kid who showed all due deference to my elders and constant regard for my teammates and fellow students. But there was the other side; my double life had begun.

In an article in June 2009, Jennifer Starks of the *Contra Costa Times* aptly captured the predicament I put myself in 20 years earlier: "O'Brien tried his first beer at 11 and began experimenting with meth as a sophomore at Pittsburg," she wrote. "The headlines may have portrayed a confident, talented athlete, but inside lived a shy teenager with low self-esteem."

"I hid a lot of things for a long time," I said in the article. "I was so accomplished, and I was always afraid of letting someone down. I lived in constant fear. I was a good kid. I worked my butt off. But there were issues inside of me. To mask them, I went to drugs. The more I accomplished, the more my drug use started compounding. It got harder and harder to get help.'"

I should have gone to Joe Aliotti or Jerry Haflich for help. A 1977 graduate of Pittsburg High and an All-American quarterback who led Boise State to the 1980 NCAA Division 1-AA national football championship, Joe was the Pirates' offensive coordinator and an assistant baseball coach when I was at Pitt. He was also friendly with my dad and Uncle Gary. Jerry, now the head football coach at American River College in Sacramento, was the defensive coordinator at PHS my senior year and is married to Aliotti's sister, Rosanne.

I grew to greatly respect and admire both Joe and Jerry as men and coaches and developed close friendships with them after I graduated from Pitt. In fact, I am godfather to Jerry and Rosanne's daughter, Whitney, who is now in her early 20s.

In 1994, my senior season at BSU, I switched my uniform number from 55 to 14, Joe's number with the Broncos, in his honor. (I admit, 14 is an odd number for a defensive end, but it was good karma: Following in Joe's footsteps from Pittsburg to Boise, I, too, was a team leader, earned first-team All-America and Big Sky Conference Player of the Year honors, and played for the 1-AA national title.)

Like almost everyone else at PHS, Joe had no idea I had a problem. "I wish he would have come to me for help," said Aliotti, who is now dean of students at De La Salle High School in Concord, California. "There were a lot of people who loved and admired Joe. He's a good person with a good heart. I knew about his battles with his dad, so to be honest I know he lacked some guidance at times, but I had no idea about his involvement with drugs. He was a great kid and a classy young man when he was in high school. I thought we had the kind of relationship where he could come to me with any problems back then. He was about 16, so that would have made me about 30. That's why I was hurt when I found out about the trouble he got into later in his life. After learning about his arrest I was disappointed. No, that's not a strong enough word: I'd say I felt shocked, betrayed and hurt."

I've talked to Aliotti a few times since my arrest, and it's never been the same, though I understand his disappointment. I was too ashamed and afraid to seek Joe's counsel when I was in high school because I looked up to him so much. Moreover, I didn't want to disappoint the people who looked up to me. It was my own fault for not seeking help, and my problem only got worse. I fell further into the abyss of the dual life I was creating—an existence where it took as much effort to hide the secret of my drug use as it did to excel on the football field. Because so many people looked up to me, my fear of getting caught as a drug user, which would in turn label me a failure as an athlete, became both the motivation for and the destructive force behind my entire existence.

Still, I was able to conceal the dissolute part of my life from almost everyone. I wasn't a street addict and I never looked like the strung-out, pockmarked users portrayed on the anti-meth TV commercials, all of which helped me live The Lie. I cruised through my senior year under the guise of a model student-athlete and a solid citizen—wooed by college recruiters and honored with dozens of awards for my leadership, civic-mindedness, academic excellence and athletic prowess—but I was also a meth user, trapped in my own duplicity because I couldn't bring myself to disappoint those who saw me as a leader and role model. It was incredibly hard, but I was used to doing things the hard way.

MY USE OF meth would eventually take me down a path of near oblivion and disgrace. But at the time I thought I was invincible—a well-conditioned, powerfully built athlete destined to be a college football standout. Because I was young, in excellent shape, and didn't snort meth on a daily basis, I fooled myself into believing I didn't have a drug problem and that my body could deal with the occasional impurities I was ingesting. Football, not drugs, I told myself, was still my passion. Despite the storm that loomed overhead, I had no doubt that I was going to play college football. In fact, as I considered the initial offers from the various teams that contacted me, I had visions of playing for a big-time program, perhaps a Pac-10 school. But my height would be my Achilles' heel and haunt me throughout my playing career. "Joe O'Brien came into his own as one of the better linemen on both sides of the ball in the BVAL," the *Pittsburg Post-Dispatch* said after my senior season. "The thing hurting O'Brien is his height. He's 6-2, 240."

"Every coach says I'm one inch too short," I told the newspaper. "My play is fine and my grades are all there. I'm just one inch too short. But one thing they don't realize is I just turned 17 in November, so I'm still growing. I thought that would work to my advantage, but it hasn't."

And it never did. When the time came for me to choose a college, all but a few of the schools that expressed an initial interest in me—Cal among them—made a formal scholarship offer when it seemed my height was not going to exceed 6-2, which, in their judgment, was too short for a lineman.

The University of Nevada informed me that if I were one inch taller it "would take me right now," I told the *Post-Dispatch*. "It seems silly that they don't look at the quality of the player." My high school teammate Steve Hines, agreed. "I think Joe could have played in the Pac-10, but they thought he was too small," he said in the same article. "But you watch, Joe is like a flower who is going to blossom later." My top suitors turned out to be three northern California schools—Santa Clara, St. Mary's and Sacramento State.

Choosing a school was a tough decision, and I could have used my father's counsel. But again, he wasn't there for me; he died the previous October.

EACH THURSDAY EVENING before Pittsburg High's Friday night football games, my dad, Uncle Gary, Aunt Dina and I had a weekly ritual where we would host a spaghetti dinner for some of my teammates at Gary and Dina's home. The guys and my relatives and I would have an enjoyable meal, then my teammates and I would sit down and watch the film from our game the previous week to help prepare for the next night's contest.

On this particular Thursday evening, Oct. 5, 1989, as we got ready for our fifth game of the season the next night against Pinole Valley, Hines, Benji Simonton and Junior Bouchereau were among those who came over for dinner. My dad, who was a journeyman electrician for Contra Costa Electric of Pleasant Hill, and Uncle Gary, a steelworker, were no-shows, so we just assumed they had to work late and started our meal without them.

In the days leading up to that fateful evening, my dad had been acting stranger than usual. At times he was drowsy and his mental functions seemed slow and labored. I had seen this behavior before when he was doing some serious drugs. When I asked him if he was OK, he told me it was some kind of reaction to some prescription he was taking and not to worry. But I *was* worried: My father didn't do illicit drugs in front of me, but I was all too familiar with his history of substance abuse.

Just as Aunt Dina, my teammates and I sat down to dinner, the phone rang in the next room. Dina got up and answered it. About a minute later she returned to the dining room. "Joe, I need to talk to you for a minute," she said.

"Aw, c'mon Dina, I'm about to eat," I replied.

"Joe, I need to talk to you right now," she said firmly.

As I looked closer, I could see tears welling in her eyes. "You need to go across the street," she said, referring to my grandmother's house.

"What for?" I asked. "What's going on?"

"JUST GO!" she yelled.

I put my fork down, pushed myself away from the table, and nervously trotted across the street to my grandmother's house. I had a sinking feeling in my stomach that something really bad was about to happen. When I arrived, my Uncle Gary met me at the door. He was in his steel mill uniform—steel-toed boots, dark blue worker's shirt and pants—which he never wore at home. One of his fingers was heavily wrapped in fresh gauze; it was obvious he had suffered a serious cut that required medical attention, a common occurrence in his line of work. But when I saw the look on my uncle's face, I immediately knew his injury was not why he had summoned me. Still, I held out hope. "What the hell is going on here?" I asked. "Is your finger amputated?"

He didn't even bother to answer my question. "Joe," he said, "your dad's dead."

My knees nearly buckled and my entire body momentarily went numb; it felt like someone had reached in my throat, ripped out my heart, then punched me in the stomach.

MY UNCLE GARY had indeed suffered a nasty cut while working at the local steel mill and went to Pittsburg's Los Medanos Community Hospital to get stitches in his finger. As he was getting ready to leave, he heard something about an overdose and then my dad's address over the emergency room intercom. He raced out of the hospital, got in his car, and sped to our house. It was around 5 p.m. When he arrived, there was an ambulance and two or three police cars in front of the house. When he reached the front door, a cop stopped him. "You can't come in," the policeman said.

"Fuck you," Gary replied. "That's my brother in there."

"You don't want to go in there," the cop said. "He's dead—looks like a drug overdose."

After he regained his composure, Gary drove to my grandmother's, called Dina, and had her send me across the street.

My dad passed away in the bathroom of our home seconds after he did a hit of Mexican black tar heroin. We were told the amount he shot up wasn't usually fatal, but the smack he scored was part of a tainted batch that had caused a rash of overdoses in the Bay Area at that time. "O'Brien is the only East County resident known to have suffered a black tar overdose so far from the batch plaguing the Bay Area," the Antioch *Daily Ledger* reported two days later. "Pittsburg police said a batch of the drug that entered the country from Mexico last week is contaminated and has been causing problems for Bay Area heroin users. On the street, black tar sells for about $20 for two-tenths of an ounce. Police said O'Brien injected less than that Thursday. Three people died in San Francisco and about 50 others were treated for overdoses caused by the gooey black drug."

Uncle Gary and I later figured my dad had been doing heroin for a few months before he died. We knew he took drugs, but we had no idea that he had added smack to his indulgences. "In my wildest dreams I would never think something like that would happen," I told the *Post-Dispatch* a week or so later. "It shocked me; it shocked my uncle."

Given the popularity of Pitt football in my hometown, my personal tragedy became a public affair as the *Post-Dispatch* wrote a lengthy article about my loss. "Young Pirate learning to deal with father's death," the headline read. "I was probably the closest person to my father," I told the paper's Larry Espinola. "We were close friends. I never will understand. The first couple of days I was more mad at him than sad. But I'm over the anger. I miss him so much."

FOURTEEN YEARS AFTER my father passed away, I watched Brett Favre, as he played in a nationally televised Monday night football game the day after his dad died of a heart attack, reach deep inside himself to play one of the greatest games of his career at one of the lowest points in his life.

I knew exactly what he was going through.

Favre played his aching heart out that night in Oakland as he pulled himself together and summoned up his huge competitive spirit in his dad's honor and led Green Bay to a 41-7 win over the Raiders. He shredded Oakland's defense with four touchdown passes in the first half and finished with 399 total yards.

As I watched Favre's spectacular performance on TV and read his postgame comments the next day, it brought back a flood of memories: Like me, his dad, Irv, died unexpectedly. Like me, his dad was his biggest fan and his closest friend. And like me, he chose to play a seemingly meaningless football game the next day—when actually that game had extraordinary meaning. "I knew that my dad would have wanted me to play," Favre said after the game. "I love him so much and I love this game. It's meant a great deal to me, to my dad, to my family, and I didn't expect this kind of performance. But I know he was watching tonight. ... I do not wish this on anyone. My dad has been to every game from fifth grade, and he coached me in high school. You never expect it to happen like that. I'm going to miss him. He was so instrumental not only in football, but in life."

YUP, I KNEW exactly what Favre was talking about. The night after my father died turned out to be one of the most transcendent and emotional experiences of my life as I decided to play in our game against Pinole, one of the BVAL's top teams. "I just knew in my heart that my dad would want me to go out and play in that game because that was something he really lived for every Friday night," I told the *Post-Dispatch*. "I knew it was going to be hard. He used to go to every practice, every baseball game, every wrestling meet. Sometimes he would be the only one in the stands. He lived to watch me play sports. He helped me so much."

Knowing my dad, I still know it would have been a huge mistake *not* to play that night.

I was determined to take the field against Pinole, but there were moments when I thought my grief would suffocate me. As game time approached, I felt like I was drowning in emotion and wasn't sure if I could maintain my composure even though I told my teammates I was ready to play. "I told them my dad would want us to do our best and would want me to do my best," I said in the *Post-Dispatch* article, "and I'm going to try and concentrate as much as I can to pull this game out."

The hardest part was right before the game. My dad and I had a pre-game routine where I would seek him out in the stands and give him the fist pump from the field, to which he would give me the same signal in return. That night my Uncle Gary and about 40 of Dad's friends were in the stands, some of whom gave me the fist pump before the opening kickoff. It was a moment that remains with me to this day. "I've never been scared before a football game," I said in the *Post-Dispatch* article. "It wasn't the usual butterflies. I was really scared to play that game, but then I saw [the gesture from the stands]."

Sports, especially a contact sport like football, can be incredibly cathartic. I was devastated and I never hurt so much inside as I did before that game, but at the same time I never felt more alive as we took the field against Pinole. Aroused by the events of the previous 24 hours, I played with a competitive rage I never knew I had. From the opening kickoff until I got kicked out of the game in the closing minutes for fighting, I was a man possessed, making somewhere around 20 tackles. Even though we lost 32-14, I was able to unburden myself for a couple of hours. "The outcome of the game wasn't a factor to me," I told the *Post-Dispatch*. "Before the game I told my teammates that it wasn't a win-or-lose situation, but for everyone to play their hardest and maybe we can win this for my father. I personally had the best game of my life. I can honestly say that."

The loss of my dad enhanced my dependence on and obsession with football. I used the game as an outlet for my grief and played at a high level the rest of my senior year. But in the wake of his death I became confused, anxious and angry, and I also used his demise as an excuse to continue my use of meth. Getting high, I rationalized, was my way to cope with the anger and sadness inside me. Outwardly, I was a 17-year-old who tried to act like an adult, but privately I was a frightened, hurt and messed-up kid with a substance abuse problem that would soon get out of hand. The end of my father's life from drug abuse also hastened my own downward spiral.

CHAPTER
4

MY MOTHER BRIEFLY RE-ENTERED MY LIFE when she sought custody of me shortly after Dad passed away. I turned 17 the next month, and as the initial shock of his untimely passing slowly wore off, I simply assumed I would return to the guardianship of my Uncle Gary and Aunt Dina, finish my senior year at Pitt High, and head off to college in the fall. But my mom, who lived in nearby Antioch at the time, had other ideas. "I'm sorry your father's dead," she told me over the phone. "I know you two were close. But right now, I'm concerned about your well-being; you're going to move back with me."

Seven years earlier I balked at my mother's attempt to spirit me away from Pittsburg and my father's care, and I sure as hell wasn't going to co-operate with her now. Her concern for my basic welfare was sincere, but I also knew she didn't care one bit about my education or athletic career; I needed the structure, support and direction Gary and Dina provided. "No, Mom," I replied. "It's not gonna happen. I'm staying here."

"Well, we'll see about that!" she angrily yelled into the phone. "I'm your parent, not Gary! I'll go to court if I have to!"

But Gary beat her to the punch; he filed an appeal for temporary custody, noting that he had been my legal guardian once before when Dad was in prison. In the investigation, the caseworker asked me where I stood on the issue. I said there was no way in hell I would rejoin my mother. I knew my response made her furious, but I didn't care. When we went to court and the judge ruled in Gary's favor, my mom flew into a rage, hurling threats at my uncle, me and even the judge as she was physically escorted from the courtroom. So for the second time in four years my Uncle Gary became my legal guardian; I lived with him, Dina and my grandmother until I departed for college the following August.

IN FEBRUARY 1990 Gary, Dina and I, along with my teammate Steve Hines and his father, Steve Sr., were featured in the *Pittsburg Post-Dispatch* when Steve and I formally received college football scholarships on national letter of intent day. "After a dinner of pasta at the home of Gary O'Brien, Joe's uncle, the two Pirate athletes signed their national letters of intent, Hines to play for Washington State University, O'Brien for Santa Clara," the article said. Although he almost certainly would have held his emotions in check, I know my dad would have been overjoyed. It was a proud yet bittersweet moment for my family members and me.

A few months later Hines, an all-conference wide receiver/defensive back who ended up playing college ball at Norfolk State in Virginia, and I were selected to play in California's 39th Shrine North-South Football Classic. Played in the Rose Bowl, the annual all-star game was a benefit for the Shriners Hospital for Children in Los Angeles and matched the top college freshmen-to-be from northern California against their counterparts from the southern part of the state.

It was a great honor; I was excited to be a part of my home state's top all-star game, which previously showcased the likes of Lynn Swann, Jim Plunkett and John Elway in one of the most famous football stadiums in the country. But I almost didn't make the trip to Pasadena: Three weeks before the game I was riding my Harley down a Pittsburg street when a dog ran in front of me. I flipped off the bike, fractured my ankle, and suffered a number of cuts and bruises. Worried that the ankle injury would preclude my participation in the game, I fibbed to the North coaches and trainers as well as to the local media, telling them it was just a severe sprain. Able to walk with just a slight limp, I made the trip to L.A. and joined my fellow all-stars the week before the game.

I also attended the various off-field activities associated with the game, including a trip with a group of coaches and players to the L.A. Shriners Hospital. Among the young patients we visited was a girl about 10 who was in the middle of a rehab session for her damaged legs. As she struggled to negotiate the therapy parallel bars, she cried in pain with each step; I noticed she had several pins in both legs, some of which oozed blood. "If you want to rest, it's OK," her therapist said. But the girl bit her lip and took another step. "No, no!" she cried. "I'm going to do this!" With impressive courage, determination and tears in her eyes, she made it to the end of the bars.

Suddenly my ankle didn't hurt as much. Later that week I told the *Post-Dispatch* how the young patients had inspired us—especially the girl with the pins in her legs. "That's why I feel good about playing in this game," I said. "And that's why we have to give 100 percent, because we're playing for [the young patients]. When I'm out here on the field, and if my legs get tired, I know it's nothing compared with what that girl is going through. It's like they say: Strong legs run so that weak legs may walk."

Most high school all-star games have a pecking order among the participants—those from the larger schools and headed to big-name colleges usually get the bulk of the media attention as well as the majority of the reps in practice—and California's 1990 Shrine Classic was no exception. With the two other North centers headed for Pac-10 schools, I was initially listed third on our team's depth chart at that position. But I wasn't about to be overlooked and, despite my bad ankle, I quickly made my presence felt on the practice field with my ferocity and quickness, earning favorable evaluations from Randy Blankenship and Mark Speckman, the North's co-head coaches. "One of the key things we heard about him was that he is real mobile and a smart kid," Speckman told the *Post-Dispatch*. "We want to go with kids that learn the fastest. We were also looking for kids that could move and had size. O'Brien fits into both those areas."

When the starting lineups were announced a few days before the game, I not only surpassed the other two players and earned the nod to start at center, but I was also selected one of the North squad's captains.

On July 28 in the Rose Bowl my high school career ended on a winning note as the North defeated the South 19-14. Hines was one of the heroes of the game with a key punt return that set up our winning touchdown in the final minute. In a tribute to my father, I played with the word "Dad" written on the tape on my wrists and the back of my helmet. "He left me at a time when things were really getting started for me with all my accomplishments," I told Larry Espinola of the *Post-Dispatch* after the game. "Sometimes when things get tough I just strive to do my best for him."

INCLUDING THE REMAINDER of my senior year at Pittsburg, I played football for another 10 seasons after my father died. And I thought about him before every game—high school, college, pros. To this day, I still mourn his passing. Despite his faults and failings—particularly the often capricious and erratic manner in which he raised me—he was my best friend and my biggest fan. Regrettably, there is no way for me to ignore his violent and dangerous lifestyle, which eventually cost him his life. But during the nearly 17 years I knew him, especially the time I lived with him in Pittsburg, his overriding message to me was: Don't do as I do, do as I say. "My uncle told me if there was one thing my dad did in his life, it was to raise me not to do the things he did," I told Espinola.

"Although the 35-year-old Scott O'Brien apparently had a relationship with drugs, he never allowed it to affect his relationship with his son," Espinola wrote. "And perhaps because he had seen the dark side of drugs, he did everything he could to make sure it never happened to his son."

I wish I could say my dad's efforts and good intentions were successful—that I heeded his admonishments and became a law-abiding adult, that I didn't take illicit drugs, didn't become violent and reckless at times, didn't have brushes with the law ... never became involved in selling drugs.

But I can't.

I don't blame either my father or mother for the troubles and entanglements I encountered during the first 30-plus years of my life. I'm culpable for the many bad decisions I have made. Sure, a normal upbringing probably would have helped, but to hold others responsible for my wrongdoings and undoing is a cop-out. "I am who I am and I did what I did, and I don't want to make any excuses about it," I told Mike Prater of the *Idaho Statesman* in June 2009. "I'm the one who makes my own decisions, and why I made those decisions? Boy, I wish I knew because I could have changed some things."

FOR THE MOST part, my early substance abuse was not habitual, nor did it adversely affect or alter my daily routine. I think that's one reason why I was able to hide it for so long. But it made me a liar. The All-American persona everyone saw was a ruse and a fabrication. I fooled them all, but I couldn't fool myself. I deceived them with my charm, my clean-cut looks, my football awards, my certificates of merit, and my ability to endure some of the hardest situations a person could live through. As I prepared to leave Pittsburg and enter college at Santa Clara, my late father's words echoed in my head: *Don't do as I do, Joe, do as I say.* But I didn't listen, and now I was lying to him, too. That, as much as anything, fills my heart with regret and remorse.

I began to take the stance of "living on the edge" and developed a "fuck everybody and everything" attitude. Eventually, I became obsessed with the need to maintain my public persona while hiding the unseemly part of my life. At first, I thought I could pull it off and blithely live my dual life without any complications or repercussions. But I was wrong. If I had sought help or gotten caught while I was still in high school or college, I may have never taken the path I did—a journey fraught with deceit and illicit activity that took me to the brink of oblivion for selling meth, getting arrested, and going to prison.

Until I got busted in 2003, I thought I had mastered living on the edge on and off the field. But I didn't realize until later the toll it had taken: I lost my ability to love myself, to appreciate the rewards of having a good heart, and to share my talents for honorable reasons. And I paid a steep price for those missteps.

A FEW WEEKS after the 1990 Shrine Classic I began my college football career at Santa Clara University of the Division II Western Football Conference. At 6-foot-2, 250 pounds, I was originally recruited to play on the offensive line as a center or guard and as the long snapper on special teams, but after one week of practice I was moved to the defensive line. Head coach Terry Malley and his staff decided my quickness, aggressiveness and intensity were better suited for the defensive side of the ball. They were right; throughout my three seasons at Santa Clara I took the field with an approach that was always hard-nosed and sometimes meanspirited. There were three primary reasons I played with such fury: First, I was angry at the world for the loss of my father. Second, the inner conflict that stemmed from my ongoing drug problem continued to create immense guilt. Third, I played with a chip on my shoulder because I thought I should have been playing at a Division 1-A school.

As a 17-year-old freshman I made my college debut at nose guard in the Broncos' 21-19 season-opening win over Chico State. I was the first true freshman to play for SCU in five years, and after I saw action in our second game, a 31-19 loss to UC Davis, I figured I would be a key contributor on the defensive line for the rest of the season. But before our third game against San Francisco State it was decided I would be better off redshirting (at the time Division II players could play up to 10 quarters before opting to redshirt), and for the rest of the 1990 season I watched from the sidelines as Santa Clara went 6-5. Even though I appeared in just two games I still practiced all season and was named the Broncos' top newcomer for 1990.

Despite the anger within me, I initially looked at my arrival at Santa Clara as an opportunity to start with a clean slate and quit my use of methamphetamine. But my renunciation of drugs was short-lived. The Santa Clara campus was more laid-back than blue-collar Pittsburg, and for those involved in the school's drug culture, hallucinogens such as marijuana, LSD and psilocybin mushrooms were more popular than street drugs such as meth. Ironically, even though I didn't particularly enjoy using marijuana in high school, I became a heavy pot smoker at Santa Clara after I realized that meth was not as readily available. Not that I stopped using my drug of choice; I still craved the flood of peace and pleasure it brought me, so I would regularly return to Pittsburg, about an hour's drive from Santa Clara, to score some "ice" or "crank" for my private use.

In 1991 I moved from reserve nose guard to starting defensive end and long snapper. My drug habit didn't hinder my ability to excel on the gridiron—at least not at first. As a redshirt freshman I led the defensive line with 71 tackles and seven sacks as the Broncos finished 5-6. One of my best games that year was in SCU's 20-18 loss to Portland State. Playing against the Vikings' All-American tackle Larry Hall, I had five tackles, two for minus yardage and one that forced a fumble. My performance that day caught the attention of then-PSU coach Pokey Allen, who would later recruit me to play for him at Boise State.

It was also in '91 that people began to recognize my potential as a coach. "What I like about Joe, besides being a good athlete, is when he comes off the field he tells me exactly what kind of blocking schemes we're seeing and what kind of defensive schemes he feels will be most effective," said Ron Modeste, Santa Clara's defensive line coach at the time. "He's an intelligent football player, and he's going to be very good when you consider that he is just a freshman right now."

Modeste and Malley also praised my passion for the game. "Joe plays very, very hard," said Modeste midway through the season. "My problem is I've got to get him out of the game to rest him once in awhile." Added Malley: "Joe is really going to be a good player for us. He's got that intensity and great strength, and his best asset is his competitiveness."

My love for football was still genuine and authentic. But as my sophomore season approached I was becoming a drug addict and The Lie was beginning to challenge my commitment. I had always pushed myself relentlessly to be a great player, but for the first time in my life I didn't work as hard in the weight room. As a redshirt freshman with D-1 talent, I usually had the upper hand on my Division II opponents during the 1991 season; I figured my natural strength and God-given aptitude for the sport would allow me to do more of the same in '92, which turned out to be the case. (One exception was when I went up against Sonoma State's massive Larry Allen, who became an 11-time All-Pro guard for the Dallas

Cowboys, one of the best run blockers in NFL history, and is a sure Hall of Famer when he becomes eligible. I had a decent game against Allen despite Santa Clara's 27-7 loss.)

I'm probably the only one who thought my performance in 1992 was substandard. When I was on the football field my competitive nature kicked in; I still practiced hard, and on Saturdays I played with my characteristic drive and determination. But there was something missing that season. Ever so slightly, I could tell my drug use was taking its toll on my mental sharpness and physical preparedness. I was smoking marijuana almost every day, snorting meth whenever I could, and mixing them both with alcohol on weekends, which led to the start of some combative behavior away from the football field. It seemed the mean streak I had on the gridiron sometimes manifested itself in social settings where the liquor flowed, especially if I was already on meth or another drug. I didn't go looking for trouble, but I got into my share of booze-fueled brawls at parties and bars while I was at Santa Clara and later at Boise State.

On the field at SCU I went to a few practices under the influence of weed, but I never missed any practices or meetings and none of my teammates or coaches suspected a thing. In fact, at the start of the 1992 season I was selected as one of Santa Clara's two defensive captains, marking the first time in the long history of the program that a sophomore had received such an honor. (Another standout underclassman for the Broncos that year was freshman basketball player Steve Nash; we became friends during the one year we overlapped at SCU.) That fall I registered more than 50 tackles and was named the Defensive Lineman of the Year by the Northern California Football Writers Association as Santa Clara finished 4-6 in what turned out to be the football program's final season.

Despite the honors I received that year, looking back I knew I could have been even better and accomplished even more had it not been for my worsening drug habit. In the back of my mind I knew what I was doing was terribly wrong and self-destructive, and the guilt created by my duplicity kept building inside me. But I didn't stop. In fact, in addition to snorting meth and smoking pot, I also experimented with acid and mushrooms a few times. At the time I still had convinced myself that I was nothing more than a recreational user, that my situation was far from dire, and that the main motivation in my life was to excel as a college football player and make it to the pros. But my perspective was becoming distorted; my public life as a college football standout and my secret life as a drug user were slowly beginning to merge into a treacherous mess. The Lie was tightening its grip on me.

AFTER THE 1992 season the NCAA decreed that Division 1-A schools could no longer field Division II or III football teams and would be required to maintain a Division 1-A or 1-AA program. Of the 27 schools nationwide affected by the ruling, only Santa Clara, citing the increased costs of funding a program at a higher level, chose to eliminate football.

Although I was receiving a first-rate education at Santa Clara and the school said it would honor the remainder of my scholarship, my decision in response to its decision to scrap its football program was easy: I was going to transfer to another school and continue playing. My education was important, but at that point in my life football, despite my ongoing substance abuse, was still my top priority. I had serious aspirations to play in the NFL, and with close to 140 tackles and 14 quarterback sacks in my first two-plus collegiate seasons, I thought I had a legitimate shot to make the pros if I continued to improve, especially if I could escape the relative obscurity of Division II football.

With the announcement of the SCU football program's demise, several schools were quick to contact me, including Hawaii, Arkansas, Nevada, Oregon, Cal, Sacramento State and San Jose State. But the team that seemed to want me the most was Boise State of the Division I-AA Big Sky Conference. At the end of the '92 season Portland State's Pokey Allen was named the head coach at BSU. Although Santa Clara and PSU didn't meet in '92, Allen and his staff still remembered me from the previous year. "We were attracted to Joe when he was a freshman and we were coaching at Portland State," said Barry Sacks, Boise State's defensive line coach under Allen, in an article in the *Daily Ledger-Post Dispatch*. "We had an All-American offensive tackle and Joe was a young freshman, and Joe just chewed him up. We were saying if he can do that as a freshman, think what he's going to be like as a senior. I'm sure our offensive line coach chewed out our player for letting a freshman kick his fanny up and down the field."

Joe Aliotti's strong endorsement on my behalf certainly didn't hurt. As one of the top names in BSU football history, a member of the Broncos' Athletic Hall of Fame, and a former assistant coach at Oregon State who knew Allen and some of his assistants, his word carried a fair amount of weight. "I told Pokey and [offensive coordinator] Al Borges that Joe was a great kid," said Aliotti, an assistant coach at Pittsburg High when I played for the Pirates. "I might have helped a little by knowing some people and giving him a good recommendation, but Joe was the main reason he got the scholarship to Boise State because he was an outstanding football player."

The only time I had been to Boise was during the summer of 1992 when I worked at a high school football camp on the BSU campus with Aliotti, who was the offensive coordinator at Pitt High at the time. I remember running and stretching with the young players in Bronco Stadium and thinking, "Wow, Joe Aliotti played here. I wish I could play in a place like this." BSU's famous blue turf also intrigued me. I had never played on artificial turf, let alone a blue field; I felt faster and quicker as I ran on the springy surface. "Boy, it would be really awesome to play here," I said to myself. Little did I know that a few months later I would have the opportunity to do just that.

As I pondered my future and weighed the various offers I received, Boise State became a pretty easy choice. Allen and Sacks were quite persuasive when we spoke on the phone, and I quickly realized they were dead serious about making me one of the first additions to the team they had inherited from deposed coach Skip Hall. A few days after Santa Clara scuttled its football program, I went from the Broncos to the Broncos, leaving SCU for BSU with two years of eligibility remaining.

When I arrived in Boise a week or so later, my first direct contact with BSU was defensive ends coach Pete Kwiatkowski, who later became a fellow coach and close friend. An All-American defensive lineman for the Broncos in 1986 and '87 and inducted into BSU's Athletic Hall of Fame in 1996, Kwiatkowski would later join the Montana State coaching staff as its defensive coordinator and hire me as the Bobcats' defensive line coach in December 1999. He later returned to Boise State as the Broncos' defensive line coach under Chris Petersen and was promoted to defensive coordinator after the 2009 season. I spent my first night in Boise at Kwiatkowski's house, and the next day he walked me around BSU's campus and helped get me registered for the classes I needed.

Similar to my arrival at Santa Clara in 1990, I viewed my new surroundings as an opportunity to quit my drug habit, or at least get my substance abuse under control. "OK, nobody knows me in Boise," I said to myself. "I'm going to Boise State with a fresh start. I'm not doing any of this shit anymore. I'm tired of it. I'm going to start over and leave all the negative aspects of my life behind me." My initial intent was to return to the weight room and the practice field with a renewed purpose, earn a starting spot on the Broncos' defense, earn All-Big Sky honors, maybe receive some Division 1-AA All-America recognition, and make myself into a legitimate NFL prospect by the end of my senior season.

As Allen and his staff began to assemble the parts they would need to compete in their inaugural season at BSU, it wasn't long before I was singled out as one of the Broncos' top newcomers. "This young man is a coach's dream," Sacks told the *Daily Ledger-Post Dispatch* soon after I joined the program. "He doesn't know anything but full speed. Joe is a real student of the game. If you're going to pass protect against Joe, you better bring your lunch with you because it's a full day's work."

It was a different story, however, with many of my new teammates. When a new coaching staff takes over a college football program, there is almost always that tension and animosity between the players who were recruited by and played for the departed staff and those brought in by the new coaches—and the 1993 Boise State football team was no exception. Allen had inherited a struggling program from Hall, and I was among a handful of newcomers initially recruited by Pokey and his staff to shore up some of the team's glaring deficiencies. Hardly any of Hall's players liked me at first, but that just made me angrier and more determined to show them up. One of the few returning players with whom I became friendly was sophomore linebacker Brian Smith, who would become a close friend and later play a major role in the revival of my coaching career following my time in prison.

I started out fifth on the depth chart at defensive end when BSU's 1993 spring drills began, but by the time the season began that fall I was in the starting lineup and had clearly established myself as one of the team's top defensive performers as well as the special teams long snapper.

Although I had a good junior year individually—earning second-team All-Big Sky honors at defensive end with 68 tackles, four fumble recoveries, and 8½ sacks—the '93 Broncos struggled in our first year under Allen and finished a disappointing 3-8 overall and 1-6 in the Big Sky. I was certain, however, that our record would improve considerably the following fall. First, I was determined to go out in a blaze of glory my senior year—to play each down like it was my last. Second, we had several key players returning; on defense the list included Smith and Stefan Reid at linebacker, all four starters in the secondary—Rashid Gayle, DaWuan Miller, Tim Foley and Chris Cook—and me. Third, it was quite evident that our team had a special group of coaches—led by the colorful and charismatic Allen—who knew how to win.

During most of my first several months at Boise State I limited my indulgences to alcohol and recreational use of marijuana. But after the 1993 football season I returned to my hometown of Pittsburg for Christmas vacation and spring break; while I was there I hooked up with some of the meth users I knew. Once I started using "ice" again in 1994 I brought it back to Boise with me, and my cycle of deceit began anew: The more attention I garnered as a high-profile student-athlete at BSU, the more I found it necessary to carefully craft my illusion of self-discipline and propriety. However, there were a few occasions when I screwed up and almost blew my cover when my anger nearly got the best of me.

IT HAD BEEN more than four years since my dad's death, but I was still trying to cope with the loss and make sense of why he left me. We all grieve differently, and in my case my bouts of sadness and anger, especially when fueled by drugs and alcohol, would make life seem caustic and cruel. And it occasionally caused me to become irrational and violent.

On the football field and in the locker room at Boise State I was emerging as a popular leader, just like I had been at Pittsburg High and Santa Clara. But off campus my insolent alter ego would sometimes manifest itself when I was under the influence of drugs and/or alcohol. Like my late father, I could be a hell-raiser under the right (actually wrong) conditions, and at 250 pounds I wasn't afraid to throw my weight around. On a handful of occasions I got into bar fights and scrapes with the law; luckily, I wasn't arrested those times and evaded public scrutiny and media attention.

One altercation occurred in the spring of 1994 when I got into a fight with Glen Amador, a former Boise State wrestler and assistant coach. I was in a downtown Boise bar on a Saturday night with teammates Kimo von Oelhoffen and Puni Alefaio when Puni and a friend of Amador's got into an argument on the dance floor over a girl. Some pushing and shoving ensued, and when I waded into the fray I was all of a sudden squared off with Amador, a badass in his own right who wrestled for Boise State in the late 1980s. Neither Amador nor I had an issue with the other; we were both just protecting our friends. But we both had been drinking and neither one was going to back down. I told him to get his hands off me or I was going to fuck him up, and he responded with a similar threat and suggested we take it outside. I agreed. We walked side by side out of the bar, down an alley, and to a small park a block or so away.

"It was almost comical how calm we were," Amador recalled years later. "There wasn't any yelling, loud threats or finger pointing. We both said something like, 'Hey, if you want to fight, I'm gonna kill you, or I'm gonna knock you out.' Joe was a well-known BSU football player, so when people saw us getting ready to fight, a big crowd followed us out of the bar and quickly gathered."

I've been in my fair share of bar fights; they are brutal, no-holds-barred encounters, and this one was no exception.

"After we exchanged blows, Joe dragged me to the ground and got on top of me; he was holding my arms so I couldn't get any punches in,"

Amador said. "But I got an arm loose and got him in a headlock. Then I bit his nose."

I still have the scar on my nose to prove it. The pain from Amador's bite was so excruciating, I momentarily lost my grip, and he let loose with several punches even though we were both still prostrate on the ground.

"Joe was so strong he actually picked me and himself off the ground at the same time after I bit him," said Amador, who was in his mid-20s and weighed about 210 at the time. "I'd say the whole fight lasted four to six minutes."

The crowd quickly dispersed before the cops showed up, but Amador and I hadn't seen the last of each other.

"The next day I was at Les Bois [racetrack in Boise] with my wife, and when we arrived Joe was working as one of the parking lot valets," said Amador, who owns a health-care company in Las Vegas and dabbled in mixed martial arts as recently as 2008.

We recognized each other right away, which was pretty easy for him since I had a bandage on my nose.

"When I got out of the car, I looked at Joe and said, 'Hey, I don't want any problems. What happened downtown last night is over, right?'" Amador recalled. "I wasn't sure what was going to happen, but Joe said, 'Yeah, it's over, we're cool,' and we shook hands. He turned out to be a nice kid. After that he was a good guy to me and we stayed on good terms."

If I had been a typical 21-year-old college student, my public unruliness would have been no big deal. But I was a Boise State football player; if caught, my indiscretions, however minor, created the potential for extensive media coverage, embarrassment to the team, disciplinary action, public scorn, and, worst of all, the exposure of The Lie.

In Boise and the surrounding area, Bronco football is, was and continues to be the biggest game in town. Since its early days as a junior college power, the Boise State football program has enjoyed loyal and widespread support from the denizens of the Treasure Valley—long before the Broncos gained nationwide acclaim for their epic victory over Oklahoma in the 2007 Fiesta Bowl. Bronco football is part of Boise's fabric, and BSU players and ex-players are quasi celebrities in and around Idaho's state capital. Being a BSU football player was usually a blessing, but sometimes it could be a curse because of the microscope under which we lived.

Fortunately, my set-to with Amador didn't make the police blotter or reach the local media, and by and large I was able to keep my second life—The Lie—a secret from the general public. Thank goodness I steered clear from any bad publicity or legal woes early in 1994 because I was about to embark on the most exciting and memorable football season of my life.

FOR AS LONG as I can remember, people have called me fiery and emotional with an innate ability to inspire others—that I possess a rare gift to lead by word and example. In 1994 those skills reached their full potential at BSU. By the start of my senior season I was an undisputed leader among the '94 Broncos. Wide receiver Jarett Hausske and I were elected co-captains that spring; in turn I became a passionate and quotable team spokesman—a favorite among the local media for my willingness to grant interviews and speak my mind. I harbored no illusions that I could single-handedly change the destiny of an entire college football program, but I was determined to do my part to turn things around. Even though our team was unimpressive in 1993 and not expected to do much in 1994, I was having none of that. The '94 season marked my senior year, and I had yet to play on a team with a winning record at the college level. It was time to make a "statement."

As both a player and a coach, I always have been willing to share my opinion, and as we prepared for the '94 season I took it upon myself to exhort my teammates to shoot for what seemed all but impossible at the time: the NCAA Division 1-AA national championship.

On letterhead from the Boise State football offices dated "Summer 1994," I wrote the following note to my fellow players: "We are now entering the last stretch of our training before we strap on the pads and show the country just how Boise State football is played. I am excited about how we have jelled as a team and are all focusing on the same goal—to be NATIONAL CHAMPIONS! This goal is very obtainable but cannot be accomplished unless the intensity in our workouts throughout the summer is sustained or taken to a higher level. Work hard. I am looking forward to playing with all of you this fall."

Given our struggles the previous year and the modest expectations for the upcoming season—"Improved Broncos still lack playoff look," said an *Idaho Statesman* headline before the season began—some of my teammates probably thought I was full of hot air and my message nothing more than blustery rhetoric. But I never tried to be obtrusive or overbearing. I was a senior and a team captain, and seniors and captains are supposed to lead. I just wanted to win, and if becoming more vocal and displaying a rah-rah attitude were needed to get things going, I was more than willing to provide the impetus.

It seemed to work. As our season opener against Northeastern approached, my teammates and coaches and the media alike began to take note of my forceful personality: "Every child should have a hero like Boise State football player Joe O'Brien," wrote Mike Prater of the *Idaho Statesman*. "And every football team should have a defensive end like Joe O'Brien. Is this guy for real or what? 'I want my son Philip to grow up just like him. I love him to death,' BSU defensive line coach Barry Sacks said. 'Normally I don't talk about one of my players in public like that, but this guy is special.'"

On the football field and in front of the media I said and did the right things. I had become a primary spokesman for our team and the face of Bronco football in 1994. But I didn't really enjoy it as much as I should have because of all the guilt and pain I carried inside me.

"Even the offensive linemen O'Brien beats up every day in practice are in awe," Prater continued in his article. "'I have two inspirations on this team, and one is Joe O'Brien,' said 6-5, 285-pound offensive tackle Keith Jeffery, who lined up against the 6-2, 248 O'Brien during two-a-days. 'He kicks my butt every day, then pats me on the butt and tells me how to counter it. The guy is absolutely amazing. If I played on a football team of Joe O'Briens, we wouldn't lose a game.'

"O'Brien's inner strength is a fierce inner-drive and an equally strong work ethic," Prater continued. "He's not the biggest guy on the team, nor is he the fastest. 'He's not a great talent by any means,' head coach Pokey

Allen said, 'but he works hard on every play. You'll never catch Joe screwing around.'"

In an interview in 2010, Brian Smith, a leader in his own right, recalled the "vision" I seemed to possess that autumn 16 years earlier. "Even before the season began, Joe seemed to know what it would take to reach the heights we did," said Smith, who received All-Big Sky second-team honors in 1994 and '95. "His leadership was paramount to us reaching the level we did that year. He got us all on the same page and got us to reach our highest capacity. It was Joe's vision that helped us make it that far. He led by word and example. The work ethic he displayed that year was inspirational."

Flattering words indeed. But it just made me more paranoid about being able to conceal my "other" life from my coaches and teammates and the Boise general public. Because The Lie became so much a part of every decision I made, my duplicity became second nature. While I talked a good game about the effort and unity needed to win football games, I was slowly, inexorably straying down a path of drug-induced ruin.

Nevertheless, I'd like to think that some of the leadership, intensity and dedication—the qualities so many others raved about—that I displayed that fall and early winter played a role in the Broncos' success in 1994, which turned out to be one of the greatest and most exciting football campaigns in Boise State history—right up there with the Joe Aliotti-led Division 1-AA national championship season in 1980 and the Broncos' undefeated, Fiesta Bowl-winning years in 2006 and '09.

Let's get one thing straight: Bronco fans who saw me perform for BSU in 1994 saw the *real* Joe O'Brien on the gridiron. The team needed me, Pokey and his coaching staff were counting on me, and it was time for me to step up. What I did on the field was genuine; I played every down like it was my last and I competed solely for the love of the game. It was during those contests that I was able to lose myself in the moment and forget my problems. It was football, pure and real.

Despite preseason predictions that had Boise State among the Big Sky Conference's also-rans, the '94 Broncos won their first six games before losing to Idaho State 32-31 in Pocatello. After that game I made a bold prediction. "This team will bounce back," I told the *Idaho Statesman*. "We'll work our butts off, and we'll sweep the rest of our games."

It turned out I was right. Boise State won the rest of its regular-season contests and clinched the program's first league championship in 14 years in the regular-season finale with a pulsating 27-24 win over archrival Idaho. The memorable victory in Bronco Stadium also ended a vexing 12-game losing streak to the Vandals.

The week before we hosted Idaho, I stirred up the already heated rivalry when I guaranteed a Boise State victory. In the emotional moments after the game, two of our offensive stars, wide receiver Ryan Ikebe and quarterback Tony Hilde, who hooked up for three touchdowns in the win, pointed to my leadership as a key factor in both the game's outcome and the team's overall success. "What can you say about the guy? You can't get any better of a leader than Joe O'Brien," said Ikebe. Added Hilde: "Joe has a big heart, and heart goes a long way. Joe knows what he wants and he pushed us all year, including today. He's our inspiration." My teammates' praise and our success helped me stay focused that fall; at the time The Lie was in the background, but it was never completely out of the picture.

We qualified for the Division 1-AA playoffs and won three hard-fought, thrilling contests in Bronco Stadium to advance to the championship game against Youngstown State. We lost to the Penguins 28-14, falling just short of the unlikely goal I helped set at the start of the season—a pipe dream that almost came true.

CHAPTER
5

WITH ITS MEMORABLE REGULAR SEASON and astounding 1-AA playoff run, Boise State's 1994 football campaign was the most rewarding athletic experience of my life. Many of my teammates have remained lifelong friends, and from that unforgettable autumn we share something that will last for the rest of our lives.

One of those former teammates is Brian Smith. "We were like a family," he said of the '94 Broncos. "I've been involved in football as a coach and player for a long time. I've been around guys from programs like Alabama, Florida State and USC; I've heard their stories, but they've got nothing on what we experienced—the tightness and the friendships—on that 1994 team at Boise State. That '94 season was an extraordinary experience."

From an individual standpoint, the '94 season was equally gratifying: I received first-team All-America honors from both the American Football Coaches Association and the Associated Press in Division 1-AA (now called the Football Championship Subdivision) and was named first team all-conference and the Big Sky Defensive Player of the Year.

But the personal accolades and team accomplishments I enjoyed in '94 mattered little a few days after the season ended when Pokey Allen was diagnosed with a rare and deadly tissue cancer.

My teammates and I were rocked by the news of Pokey's illness, but he told me not to worry and urged me to focus my energy on my goal to play pro football. In my zeal to make it to the NFL I made conditioning and weightlifting my top priority and full-time occupation. I stopped going to classes at BSU but still collected my athletic scholarship funding and continued to use the weight room and training facilities in the Broncos' Varsity Center, bulking up to 265 pounds by early 1995.

I wasn't invited to the NFL combine that February, but I hoped my credentials as a consensus All-American, my reputation as an aggressive, intense player, and the handful of pro tryouts I participated in would pique the interest of at least a few teams. In addition, I signed with sports agent Kyle Rote Jr., the former professional soccer star and founder and CEO of Athletic Resource Management Inc.

As draft day '95 approached, I wasn't sure where I stood in the eyes of the NFL until I got a call from Minnesota Vikings special teams coach Gary Zauner a few days before the draft. "Joe, we love your aggressiveness," he said, "and we love what you do as a long snapper, but we don't need a D-lineman. We need a tight end who can block. Can you catch the ball?"

I was never a receiver, but that hardly mattered. "Of course I can," I replied. "Absolutely."

Zauner said he needed some videotape showing my pass-catching ability right away, so the next day I got Boise State quarterback Tony Hilde and a member of the athletic department's video crew to help me. For about 40 minutes as the videotape rolled I ran a variety of pass routes on Bronco Stadium's blue turf and caught almost all of Tony's accurate throws. I shipped the tape to Zauner at the Vikings' football offices the same day.

I knew I wasn't going to get picked the first day of the draft, but given the interest Minnesota showed in me, I thought there was a decent chance I'd go on the second day, especially since the Vikings had two picks in the seventh (and final) round. With bated breath, I kept a close eye on ESPN's coverage of the draft's second day with some friends in my Boise apartment, hoping to have a small celebration if and when the Vikings (or any other team, for that matter) called my name. But when the seventh-round picks were announced, Minnesota chose two other defensive linemen— Jose White of Howard University and Jason Fisk, who played for Vikings coach Dennis Green at Stanford before Green took the head coaching job at Minnesota.

I was terribly disappointed, but that evening I got a phone call from Zauner. "Joe, we want to bring you to Minnesota," he said. "But first you have to try out for us. If you do OK, we might sign you as a free agent. Can you leave tomorrow?"

"Sure, I can leave tomorrow," I said, trying not to sound like I was ready to explode with excitement.

When I arrived at the Vikings' training facility in Eden Prairie, Minnesota, Zauner said they still wanted me to try out at long snapper and tight end. Under the watchful eyes of Green, Zauner, defensive coordinator Tony Dungy, and other coaches and scouts, I went through a battery of tests and drills with several other hopefuls, both draft picks and undrafted free agents. I ran a series of drills alongside defensive tackle John Randle, caught passes from quarterback Warren Moon, and did some long snapping, all of which I thought went quite well. So did Dungy. "O'Brien, we're very impressed with you," he said after my workout. "Very good job." A few minutes later I was sitting in the locker room when a member of the staff approached me and said Green wanted to see me in his office.

I quickly showered, got dressed and hurried to Green's office. My heart was pounding like crazy, my stomach was churning, and my mind was racing. I had been waiting for this moment since I was a kid, and now I didn't know what to expect or how to prepare myself. Although I was pleased with my performance in the tryouts, I wasn't sure what kind of impression I had made on Green and the others. Had Green summoned me just to send me packing, or was my dream about to come true? I gave myself a little pep talk: "OK, get a grip, and don't get your hopes up. It's not the end of the world if this doesn't work out." When I walked into Green's office he was watching highlights of some of my games at Boise

State. "Hey, that's a good sign," I said to myself. "He's taking the time to watch me on film."

"Have a seat, Joe," Green said as he played and replayed a couple of my better tackles. "You're impressive on film—good pursuit, good form. Tell me, why did you wear number 14?"

"I switched numbers my senior year to honor my friend Joe Aliotti," I replied, hoping I wasn't babbling, giving stupid answers, or wasting his time. "He was an All-American quarterback at Boise State before me; I also played for the same high school he did, and he coached me in high school."

He nodded and again turned his attention to the VCR. My heart was beating so loud, I wondered if Green could hear it. With the tape playing in the background, we spent a few more minutes talking about my professional goals and aspirations as well as the Vikings' future plans. Finally he said, "Tell me, Joe, why should the Minnesota Vikings sign you to a contract?"

I gulped. "Well, Coach, in addition to my ability, I have a really strong work ethic, I have leadership skills, and I think I'm a smart player. In fact, I want to be a coach when my playing career is over."

Green again glanced at the VCR and the unusual image of a defensive end wearing number 14. Then he looked at me as if he was mulling his decision and still needed convincing. "Most of all, I love playing football," I added. "It's the most important thing in my life; I can promise you, I will give everything I have to make this team."

With that, he stood up and extended his hand. "That's good enough for me. Congratulations, you're a Minnesota Viking."

I jumped to my feet and grabbed his hand. "Thank you," I breathed.

"Talk to your agent," Green said. "For now you'll get the minimum signing bonus, $2,000, and a training camp salary, and of course we'll pay to move you here. You're going to have to work your ass off to make this team. If you make the cut, it will mostly be because of your ability as a long snapper. Anything else you can do for us will be a bonus. We thought about you as a tight end, but as of right now you're a defensive lineman."

"Whatever you say, Coach," I replied. "I'll do my best."

What I liked about Green was that he didn't make an issue of my height. In fact, I was the same height and close to the same weight as Randle, who at the time was one of the best defensive linemen in the NFL and was later enshrined in the Pro Football Hall of Fame.

As I walked out of Green's office, my mind was awash with emotion. I thought I deserved a shot at the NFL, and if given the opportunity I thought I would succeed. But when it actually happened it felt surreal. When I was alone, I stopped and said to myself, "Wow, this is real. This really happened." And I broke down.

I REPORTED TO the Vikings' training camp in Mankato, Minnesota, in late July and was listed among the reserve down linemen and as the number two long snapper behind veteran Mike Morris. At first I was somewhat starstruck as I toiled with All-Pros such as Randle, Moon and wide receiver Cris Carter. But my elation and excitement over the chance to play professional football was quickly tempered by the inevitable pain and drudgery of a typical NFL summer camp: The two-a-day workouts were brutal and exhausting, the Midwest summer heat and humidity were oppressive, and as an undersized, free-agent rookie from a Division 1-AA school, I wasn't feeling the love from my new teammates. "Being a rookie who's not supposed to be here, guys look down on you, thinking you're not worth a damn," I told the *Idaho Statesman* a week or so after camp started. "You get zero respect. You're lower than dirt. But I'm not a quitter, obviously, so I battled through it."

To help with that battle, I turned to the painkillers. My use of pain pills was relatively brief, and I certainly was no neophyte to the medicinal benefits of certain pharmaceuticals. But my exposure to the way NFL players used pills to help cope with the pain and exhaustion inherent in their line of work was an eye-opener—and I took full advantage of it since I was a long way from my meth sources in California and Idaho. During training camp I'd throw down several pain pills in the morning to help manage the arduous workouts that day, then take downers after practice to ease the soreness and deal with the fatigue. It was a daily ritual that left me restless and edgy. In the mornings after just a few hours of sleep

I'd wake up and think, "Oh, my God, I've got to do this again?" But then the pills would quickly ease my angst, and the muggy weather seemed to amplify their pleasant buzz. For much of the time I was in Mankato, I felt like I was in some kind of steamy haze.

I was generally pleased with my overall performance in the Vikings' camp and tried not to fret about the possibility of getting cut. With the help of the painkillers in my system, I approached each practice session and scrimmage with my usual intensity and refused to back down when tempers flared, which they inevitably do in the sweltering heat. In my mind I said, "Fuck these guys. I'm going 100 miles per hour, and if you don't like it, screw you."

I wear my heart on my sleeve, so it was no surprise that I could barely keep my emotions in check a few weeks later as I got ready to play in my first professional game, a preseason Monday night contest in San Diego. "I broke down before the game in the locker room," I told the *Statesman*. "It was so weird. Coach Green was talking, and as I looked around at all the football players, I realized I was one of them now. I've never had goose bumps in my cheeks before. It was overwhelming."

With a dozen friends and family members watching from the stands, I entered the Vikings' exhibition opener at defensive tackle in the second quarter and performed reasonably well against the Chargers, finishing with four tackles and half a quarterback sack in the nationally televised game, which Minnesota won 23-19. Based on my pro debut I thought my chances of sticking with the Vikings were pretty good, but then my playing time inexplicably began to dwindle. In Minnesota's next game at New England I played about one quarter, and in the third game at home against the Raiders I didn't play at all. It didn't take me very long to realize the obvious: The Vikings simply had too many defensive linemen and Morris remained a fixture at long snapper; I was released near the end of training camp.

Despite my deep disappointment, I remained optimistic that I would catch on with another NFL team, primarily because of my long-snapping skills. But when the British Columbia Lions of the Canadian Football League contacted me, I suddenly found myself at a crossroads. I wanted to play pro football, but I wasn't sure the CFL was the answer. Furthermore, I had developed painful bone spurs in my ankle, and I was quite certain I would require surgery before I could play at full speed. Unsure of what to do, I decided to call Pokey Allen. He had played in the CFL in the mid-1960s and could certainly give me some good advice.

WHEN I CONTACTED Pokey by phone I knew he had undergone serious cancer treatments earlier that spring and summer, but I had no idea how dire his condition was when I reached him at his office at Boise State. From the weakness in his voice, it was obvious he was quite ill—recovering from a harrowing stem-cell transplant that nearly killed him, I learned later, as well as radiation treatment and chemotherapy—yet he was at the BSU Varsity Center with his players and coaches for fall camp, which had started a few days earlier. Near the end of our conversation, I asked his advice.

"Coach," I said, "I have a possible deal with the B.C. Lions. I don't know what to do. I still think I have a shot to play in the NFL, but if I don't get another chance there, maybe I should consider Canada. Or maybe I should just concentrate on learning how to coach."

"Hell, Joe, you don't want to play in the CFL," Pokey replied. "The pay is low and the league is shaky. Do you want to coach or do you still want to play?"

"I guess I'd like to coach now and take another shot at the NFL. But first, I think I need to get the bone spurs in my ankle fixed."

"Well, you can coach for me this season."

"Really?!"

"You don't have your degree yet, do you?"

"Uh, no."

"So that means you can't be a GA [graduate assistant], and volunteer coaches are against the rules. Tell you what, I'll hire you and pay you one dollar."

That's how my coaching career began. A few days later I returned to Boise and started out working for offensive line coach Dave Stromswold; later I assisted Barry Sacks on the D-line. Despite my drug habit, I had reached another goal and found myself moving forward professionally. The university had yet to notice that had I accepted my scholarship money but didn't take classes the previous spring, so I still had a solid reputation within the BSU community. Moreover, I took the necessary precautions to keep The Lie a secret, although the meth and other drugs were never far away.

POKEY'S HEALTH IMPROVED somewhat as the 1995 season progressed, but he was never completely healthy and the Broncos were unable to recapture the magic of '94, finishing 7-4 that fall. Among the players on BSU's '95 roster was running back Tommy Edwards, a highly touted transfer from Virginia Tech.

A few hours before our season opener at Utah State, I was walking through the parking lot outside Romney Stadium with some fellow coaches when we ran into Tommy's parents. They and their two daughters had traveled from their home in Radford, Virginia, to attend Tommy's BSU debut as well as the Broncos' home opener the following weekend against Sam Houston State. As the other coaches and I visited with Tommy's parents, a petite, attractive blonde joined the group. She introduced herself as Tommy's sister Tara.

Tara and I immediately hit if off. We were close in age and she had recently graduated from James Madison University. I could tell right away Tara was more than just a casual fan. Her dad, Ken, was a star fullback at Virginia Tech in the late 1960s and was drafted by the Buffalo Bills. Her brother was a high school standout in Radford and scored 11 touchdowns as a redshirt freshman at Virginia Tech in 1993.

My most vivid memory of that first meeting was Tara's sweet smell. I don't know what kind of perfume she wore, but it was the most pleasant fragrance I had ever inhaled. I was entranced, but there was the small matter of the football game at hand, and once we said our goodbyes I didn't give our brief encounter any more thought—until we crossed paths again a few days later.

On the Monday or Tuesday after Boise State's 38-14 win over Utah State, my first game as a coach, I was alone in the film room of the BSU

Varsity Center breaking down tapes for the upcoming game against Sam Houston State. As I played and replayed the videos and pored over my notes, the door behind me opened. Assuming it was another coach or a player, I didn't bother to look and see who had entered the darkened room. But when I got a whiff of that captivating scent, I knew it was Tara—even before I turned around to see her standing in the doorway.

"Coach O'Brien, do you remember me?" she said. "I'm Tara Edwards. We met a couple of days ago at the Utah State game." She caught me slightly off guard. "Uh, sure," I replied. "Of course I remember you." A few awkward moments passed. "Need some help?" she finally asked.

I was both flattered and infatuated, but I had several hours of intense work—film, practice and meetings—ahead of me. "Gee, thanks, but I'm kinda busy and I don't think you can help me. I'm breaking down tape for our game on Saturday."

"Well, I'm going to help you anyway," she said. "I know how this works. I worked at JMU's football facility and watched this being done before."

I was almost speechless. "Um, OK. Have a seat. ... Here's what I have to do."

For the rest of the morning and into the afternoon we sat together as she helped me analyze the tapes. She actually knew what she was talking about and was quite helpful. As we talked, we quickly discovered that we had a lot of similarities and the same outlook on life. That night we went on our first date.

Tara and I kept in touch via phone after she went back to Virginia with her parents and sister, but I really wasn't sure when—or even if—we would see each other again. I made it clear to her my coaching job at Boise State that fall was a temporary gig and my primary objective was to play in the NFL. For the foreseeable future, I told her, I would probably live a nomadic life—an existence filled with uncertainty and little guarantee that I would attain the glamour and wealth often associated with being a pro football player. Tara reminded me more than once that she came from a football family and assured me she understood the time constraints and commitments of my chosen field.

I LEARNED A lot and thoroughly enjoyed my first year of coaching with Pokey Allen and his staff, and I threw myself into my job. But away from the field and the locker room I continued to struggle with The Lie. I was in constant torment because of my dual life, which at times made me malevolent and confrontational, even when I was sober.

For example, I had an altercation with some University of Idaho fans in a Boise hotel bar when they were the customers and I was the server. With my one dollar coaching salary I needed another source of income in '95, so I also worked as a bartender. One Saturday I had the evening off from my coaching duties and was working the bar alone. The manager had left for the day and the establishment was practically empty when a group of five or six Vandal boosters walked in, sat at a table, and said they wanted to watch the Idaho football game on the bar's big-screen TV. But since my boss wasn't around, I decided to enforce my own personal anti-Vandal policy.

"Ain't no Idaho games televised here," I said.

"What do you mean?" one of the men in the group responded. "We have about 15 people coming in to watch the game here."

"Well, then you better go somewhere else," I replied. "Ain't no Vandal games televised here."

"Uh, wrong," he said. "We're not going anywhere else."

"OK, I'll tell you what," I answered. "There's a TV over there in the corner. You can watch it there."

"No. We want to watch it on the big screen."

"Well, then you better go somewhere else."

"I want to see the manager," he demanded.

"He's not here," I replied. "It's just me."

Then the guy recognized me. "Oh, you're Joe O'Brien," he said. "You're that bigmouth piece of shit who guaranteed a BSU victory last year."

"Yeah, that's me," I said, "and that's exactly what we did. Now, do you guys want to order something or not? Otherwise get the fuck out of here because you're not watching your game on the big TV."

Some more vulgarities and threats were exchanged. One guy was especially mouthy, so I walked around the bar and decked him. Two others jumped me and wrestled me to the floor. I punched another guy as I got to my feet. Knowing this wouldn't go over well with the hotel's management, I took off my apron, threw it on the bar, and went home.

Less than an hour later a Boise cop showed up at my apartment. "I've got a complaint against you," he said, "and I know about your reputation. Now, I can use my discretion. If you're going to lie to me and be an asshole and give me any trouble, I can lock you up for felony assault. If you cooperate and don't give me any shit, I can give you a ticket and you won't have to come in with me. You can show up to court later and deal with it then."

I decided it would be ill-advised to argue with the officer, so I told him what happened. He cited me for a misdemeanor assault, but I again avoided the public eye and escaped with a slap on the wrist. All told, I think I had to make three court appearances in Boise for various infractions, but my wrongdoings weren't reported in the local media during my time as a player or as an assistant coach.

THERE WAS ANOTHER episode in 1995 that was also not drug-related, but an example of my reckless and rash attitude. I'm not proud of it, but as an assistant coach I actually started a fight between some Idaho State and Boise State football players following the game between the two teams that fall.

The previous year Idaho State handed our team its lone regular-season defeat when it rallied from a 15-point deficit in the final 18 minutes to pull off a 32-31 upset in Pocatello. When the game ended, an ISU player came running up to Pokey, got in his face and pushed him in the chest, yelling something like, "Yeah! We beat your ass!" I was walking off the field at Holt Arena and didn't see the confrontation.

But it was caught on film, and I saw it for the first time the following year as the other defensive coaches and I were preparing for our upcoming contest against the Bengals. We just happened to be watching the moments after the previous season's game when the image of the ISU player screaming in Allen's face and pushing him appeared on the screen.

"I remember that!" Barry Sacks said as we replayed the incident a number of times. "What an asshole! I can't believe that guy did that to Pokey! For chrissakes, Pokey's got cancer and just lost a game, and that asshole is pushing him!" Then Sacks muttered to no one in particular: "Someone should teach that guy a lesson."

That's all I needed. I checked the ISU roster and determined that the player in question was on the Bengals' 1995 squad and would be part of the team coming to Boise that week. In the closing moments of BSU's 27-17 win in Bronco Stadium the following Saturday I stood on the sidelines, took off my headset, looked at Pete Kwiatkowski and said, "I'm going to fuck him up."

I never discussed my intentions with anyone, but Pete seemed to know what I was talking about. "Joe, the game's over, forget about it," he said. "Don't do anything stupid."

But I didn't heed Kwiatkowski's warning. "I don't give a fuck," I said. "I'm beating his ass right now for pushing Pokey last year."

At the end of the game as the players and coaches mingled at midfield for the traditional postgame handshakes, I saw my target. Just as I was about to walk past him, I looked around to make sure no other coaches, on either team, were nearby. As I walked past the unsuspecting player I sized him up, caught him with a forearm shiver to the side of his helmet, and knocked him to the blue turf. I quickly moved on, but a scuffle involving a handful of players ensued. Fortunately for me, no one witnessed my assault, including the *Idaho Statesman*'s Mike Prater, who saw *something*, but could not determine who or what had initiated the fight. "Two teams with plenty of hate for each other traded turnovers and punches," he wrote in his article. "Then, with 23,621 fans heading home, it really got interesting. After the game, there was a melee of emotions as players exchanged words and elbows before coaches intervened."

When our team finally gathered in the locker room, Pokey was really pissed. "What the hell happened out there?!" he yelled. "Who the hell started that fight?! This fuckin' team is out of control! Goddamn it, I want to know what happened!"

Nobody said anything; the locker room was silent for a few minutes, but to me it seemed like I sat there staring at the floor for hours. And although they didn't see my hit, I figured Kwiatkowski and Sacks knew what happened.

About 30 minutes later as the coaches were preparing to leave the stadium and attend our traditional postgame gathering at Buster's, a local sports bar, Sacks came up to me. "Joe," he said, "*you* did it, didn't you? You gotta tell Pokey what happened."

"Jesus, Barry," I replied, "I did it because you got me all fired up."

"All the same, Pokey needs to know. He thinks some of the players started it. Somebody's going to get suspended if you don't come forward."

"Oh shit, do you think he'll fire me?"

"I don't know."

When we arrived at Buster's, the coaches and a large group of boosters had taken over several tables; the celebration was loud and boisterous. Although Pokey was in attendance, he was in the throes of his battle with cancer and wasn't in much of a partying mood those days. He sat quietly nursing a beer. Scared as hell, I grabbed a seat next to him.

I leaned toward him so no one could hear our conversation. "Coach," I said, "I need to tell you: I coldcocked that motherfucker. He's the guy who pushed you last year after they beat us."

Pokey gave me an incredulous look. "You're shitting me!" he said. "What the hell's wrong with you, Joe? You're a goddamn coach, for chrissakes! You can't be doing that shit! I don't need you taking shots at opposing players. Besides, I can fight my own battles."

He quickly calmed down and looked me straight in the eye. "Jesus, Joe, don't ever do that again." Then he called to our waitress, pointed at me and said, "Get this guy a beer."

POKEY ALLEN WAS a great coach, an exceptional man, and a major influence in my career. In August 1996 his cancer returned and forced him to take a medical leave of absence. With his days numbered, he coached the final two games of the '96 season. Five weeks after his last game on the sidelines for the Broncos, he died in his hometown of Missoula, Montana.

I took it hard. I still do. When I attended Pokey's funeral in Missoula on New Year's Day 1997, I thought about how I had hidden my secret from him—how he would have helped me without reservation. But I didn't say a word because he was dying and I thought he deserved better. I thought about how I would have disappointed him and how I wanted so much to make him proud of me. I still do.

I still can.

CHAPTER
6

YOU'RE STRONG, YOU'RE TENACIOUS, you're smart, you're fundamentally sound … but. There was always that dreaded, damnable "but." From my tryout with the Minnesota Vikings in 1995 through my final season in arena football in 1998, I regularly received positive feedback and words of encouragement from the pro coaches and scouts with whom I came in contact: *Joe, you've got the athletic ability and heart to play in the NFL,* they would tell me. Then the cursed "but" would invariably follow: *But you're just not quite tall enough to be a defensive lineman in this league.*

My height, or lack thereof in the estimation of most NFL teams, was a constant source of annoyance and frustration. However, I continued to pursue my dream based, in part, on the advice of a few NFL scouts who said my long-snap skills might make my height less of an issue. Long snap speeds are measured in tenths of a second. If the snap is slow or off target, there's risk of a block. As a general rule, a 15-yard punt snap must get to the punter in no more than eight-tenths of a second. My snaps were consistently under seven-tenths. For field goals and extra points, the seven-yard snap, hold and kick should all be executed in 1.3 seconds or less;

again almost all my snaps were at or under the desired time.

After my unsuccessful bid to play for the Vikings, I decided my best bet was to earn a position with an NFL team as a long snapper, then find a way to vie for a spot on the defensive squad, whether it was at end, tackle or even inside linebacker. "I don't know if I should gain more weight to 280 pounds to play defensive tackle," I told the Antioch (California) *Ledger Dispatch* in 1995, "or get down to 245, which is a good size for an inside linebacker."

But it never seemed to matter. Whether I made myself lighter, larger, stronger or quicker, I was never quite able to find my niche with an NFL team. "Joe definitely had the tools and mindset to play in the NFL," said Pete Kwiatkowski, Boise State's defensive coordinator and my boss at Montana State when he was the Bobcats' D-coordinator. "For lots of players like him, it's a matter of being available to the right team at the right time and having a coach take notice. In Joe's case, the timing never worked in his favor."

My personal life also changed considerably after the 1995 football season. At the time Tara Edwards and I were still corresponding by phone, and I was under the impression that we were taking things slowly. But that all changed during the 1995-96 Christmas break when she accompanied her brother, Bronco running back Tommy Edwards, on his return to BSU from Virginia, showing up unannounced on my doorstep in Boise. With Tommy waiting in the car with a load of her belongings, Tara declared her love for me and said we should live together. Who was I to argue with such whimsy, passion and romance?

AROUND THE SAME time, I had surgery to remove the bone spurs that had formed in my left ankle. The operation was necessary if I wanted to continue my quest to play pro ball. In January 1996 I got a call from my agent, Kyle Rote Jr., who said the Green Bay Packers were in immediate need of a long snapper for their upcoming NFC championship game against Dallas.

"Mark Chmura [Green Bay's starting tight end and long snapper] is having back problems and is unable to long snap," Rote said. "The Packers need a backup long snapper for the playoff game this weekend and for an additional two weeks if they beat Dallas and go to the Super Bowl. How's your ankle?"

I couldn't believe the terrible timing. I would have been a perfect fit for one of the great NFL franchises that was one win from the Super Bowl. But I had to be honest. "Not very good," I replied. "I mean, it's only been three weeks since I had my surgery."

"Can you run?" Rote asked.

"I'm not sure."

"They say they're desperate. Can you walk?"

"Well, I can try."

Despite my reservations, the Packers flew me to Wisconsin for an audition at Lambeau Field. My long snaps were sharp and accurate, but I simply couldn't run because of my ankle. The Packers decided not to sign me but said they would keep me in mind if their need for a long snapper arose at a later date. I never heard from them again.

My frustration was mounting, but at the time it never entered my mind to give up my NFL dream. I decided my best bet was to market my skills in what was then the NFL's Europe-based development league—the World League of American Football. With my ankle sufficiently healed, I was drafted in the 22nd round by the league's Scottish Claymores and signed a contract in early 1996 to play that spring and early summer. "This is the best situation for me," I told the *Ledger Dispatch* after I agreed to play in Europe. "This way I'm not committed to one [NFL] team. All 30 teams can look at me, and I have a chance to raise my stock." Started in 1991, the WLAF renamed itself the NFL Europe League in 1997 and folded in 2007.

A few weeks before I was scheduled to leave for the Claymores' training camp I got a call from Rusty Tillman, the Oakland Raiders' special teams coach. "We have a possible opening for a player like you," he said. "We're looking for a center and long snapper. Are you interested?" I hadn't played center since high school, but that hardly mattered. "You've got to be kidding me!" I almost yelled into the phone. "The Raiders are my team. Just tell me when and where."

My tryout at the Raiders' training facility in Los Angeles went well, and when I finished Tillman and a couple of other coaches told me to meet them in the team offices after I showered. I wanted desperately to play for the Raiders. My dad would have been incredibly proud and pleased. But when I sat down with Tillman and the others, they had bad news: A stipulation in the agreement between the NFL and the WLAF said I had to honor my agreement with the Claymores. But that wasn't the real problem, Tillman said, since the European season ran from March through June and NFL camps opened in July. The sticking point was that NFL teams could claim only five WLAF players per year and the Raiders had already reached their allotment. "Perhaps you can be part of our allocation at a later time," Tillman told me, but it couldn't happen any sooner than the following year, he added. "Bullshit," I muttered as I left the Raiders' offices.

I also had a tryout with Tampa Bay before I joined the Claymores. Tony Dungy, newly hired from Minnesota as the Buccaneers' head coach, remembered me from the previous season when he was the Vikings' defensive coordinator and invited me to Tampa to audition for long snapper and a spot on the defensive line.

Just as my agreement with the Claymores precluded my chance to sign with Oakland, I worried that it would also dash any hope I had to earn a roster spot with Tampa Bay. Even so, I wasn't about to turn down an audition with an NFL team, and I jumped at Dungy's offer. In the back of my mind I held out hope that, given the opportunity, there was some kind of loophole that would allow me to renege on my WLAF contract and sign with the Bucs. My hope intensified when my tryout with the Bucs went better than the ones with the Vikings, Packers and Raiders. Alas, no such loophole existed, and later that spring I was on my way to Europe.

Tara moved back to Virginia when I left the States, but we got engaged when I returned that summer.

WITH FIVE MEMBERS of the Scottish Claymores having ties to the Boise State football program, the Broncos can certainly claim partial credit for Scotland's 1996 World Bowl championship: The head coach was Jim Criner, Boise State's coach from 1976-82 who led the 1980 team to the

NCAA Division 1-AA national championship. In addition, Bill Dutton, who worked for Criner at BSU, was the Claymores' defensive line coach, while receivers coach Vince Alcalde played quarterback for the Broncos in 1986-87 and was an assistant with the program from 1989-91. The other two ex-Broncos were defensive back Frank Robinson, an All-American for BSU in 1991 who also played in the NFL with Cincinnati and Denver, and me.

Established in 1995, the Claymores finished with a 2-8 record in their inaugural season. But in 1996 we went from worst to first, finishing 7-3 in the regular season for the right to host the World Bowl and then defeating the defending champ Frankfurt Galaxy 32-27 in the title game in front of more than 39,000 fans in Edinburgh, Scotland.

During my one season in Europe I met a number of relatives, including my great aunt, who lives in Glasgow, Scotland, and visited places such as Barcelona, London and Amsterdam. Unfortunately, my drinking and drug use also escalated. Compared to the strict enforcement of drug laws in the United States, western Europe's attitude toward the use and sale of illegal drugs seemed considerably more lax. I never did heroin or cocaine, but they were both relatively easy to procure in Glasgow's backstreets, and methamphetamine could actually be had in the backrooms of certain pubs. I drank with a couple of teammates almost every night, often staying out until 2 a.m., popped amphetamines before practice, and snorted meth when the opportunity presented itself.

The violence of professional football and the risky lifestyle of chemical dependence was a dangerous mix—and another step in my inevitable downfall—but I still played on, starting on the defensive line in seven of the Claymores' 11 games and serving as long snapper. I didn't accumulate a lot of impressive statistics during the regular season, but I had a good game in the World Bowl with 3½ sacks. "Some players stepped up and made some big plays," Criner said after we beat Frankfurt for the title. "Joe O'Brien was superb on defense."

I THOUGHT I might get a call from the Raiders, Packers or Buccaneers after my performance in the World Bowl, but instead the New Orleans

Saints, in need of a long snapper, beckoned when I returned from Europe.

With the start of the 1996 NFL season just a few weeks away, New Orleans special teams coach Bobby April, in his first year with the Saints after serving in the same position with the Pittsburgh Steelers, was indeed hurting for a long snapper. Chet Franklin, the Saints' personnel director, promptly signed me to a free-agent contract; I joined the team at its preseason training camp and quickly impressed April, head coach Jim Mora, and defensive coordinator Jim Haslett with my long-snapping ability and intensity at practice. With no other long snappers in the Saints' camp, I allowed myself to believe I had finally gotten the break I needed to play in the NFL. Unfortunately, after I had been at the camp for about a week, the Steelers released veteran long snapper Kendall Gammon. When Gammon became available, April decided to sign his former player and release me. I was crushed. But Franklin told me not to give up. "I want to get you back in here [next season] and give you a legitimate shot to make it," he told me before I left.

After I was cut by the Saints I got a phone call from Terry Malley, general manager for the San Jose SaberCats of the Arena Football League, who said he needed a lineman as his team was making a late-season push to make the AFL playoffs. Malley, my head coach at Santa Clara, signed me for the final two games of the '96 season and said he would offer me a contract down the road if things didn't work out with the NFL.

True to his word, Franklin signed me to a free-agent contract with New Orleans in early 1997, giving me another chance to make the team under new head coach Mike Ditka. Still determined to play in the NFL and unwilling to take no for an answer, I trained with as much fervor as ever.

In March of that year, Tara and I got married in Virginia; a few weeks later we moved into an apartment in Metairie, Louisiana, so I could be near the Saints' training facility. "I'm going there seven days a week and putting in nine-hour days," I told Larry Espinola of the *Ledger Dispatch*. "That's the way I do things." I remained hopeful that my perseverance and resolve would eventually pay off—that I would get a break sometime, somewhere. "I know I can play physically," I told Espinola. "I can't walk away now when I'm stronger and faster than ever. This just really makes me hungry. I'm going to learn every position on special teams, on the D-line, and watch films."

I was 24 and, in spite of my drug use, at the peak of my athletic skills and ability. The Lie notwithstanding, I busted my ass and did everything possible to physically improve myself as a football player: I lost five percent body fat, increased my bench press by 40 pounds to a 430-pound bench, added two inches to my vertical leap, and dropped my 20-yard dash time from 2.83 to 2.75. I attended all of the Saints' minicamps in Metairie throughout the summer of '97 and reported to training camp at 278 pounds. I was in the best shape of my life, and I did it without steroids. Given my years of substance abuse, I think it is somewhat ironic that I never took steroids. I viewed my use of meth and other drugs as a psychological need that didn't enhance my performance as an athlete. Yet I viewed those who used steroids as cheaters. I now recognize the hypocrisy.

I WAS RIPPED and ready, but I knew the harsh reality of my substance abuse—the undercurrent of The Lie—was never far from the surface. Still, I considered myself a highly functional drug user. I didn't think it hindered my ability to play football at a high level. It was my secret, and I had it "under control." I thought I was invincible.

Then I became involved with GHB.

I had never heard of "gamma hydroxy butyrate" until the summer of 1997 when a Saints teammate (I'll call him Dale) turned me on to the drug. Dale, who resided in the same apartment complex where Tara and I lived, had been using an earlier form of GHB for about five years and eventually learned how to manufacture it himself. "This stuff is fuckin' amazing," he said the first time I tried it. "It makes all your problems and all your pain disappear."

He was right. The high it gave me was magnificent, and it wasn't long before I began making GHB with Dale for our personal use. In its infancy, the drug was used by a handful of athletes and bodybuilders because of its ability to stimulate the release of growth hormones that aid in fat reduction and muscle building. Our version of the drug was the clear liquid, which made it easy to hide and transport in water and Gatorade bottles. With the exception of one chemical, all the ingredients needed to make GHB could be purchased over the counter, and for about $150 we would make seven gallons at a time. Once Dale and I concocted the drug, all we had to do was add a spoonful of the magic potion to a container of water or any other liquid. The byproduct was an incredible high that lasted four to five hours.

I've heard GHB users and former users say that the drug's high is similar to a blissful and serene opiate high. When I was on the drug, all the bad things that happened in my life didn't matter—just like Dale promised. When I started to feel stressed out about The Lie or began to worry if I was going to earn a spot on the Saints' roster, GHB would make everything mellow. With the proper dosage the drug gave me a pleasurable, relaxed and lightheaded sensation. But ingesting the right amount was critical because too much GHB can cause unconsciousness. During the Saints' 1997 training camp I made the proper adjustments I needed between my use of methamphetamine and GHB to function and stay focused (as best I could) on my goal to play in the NFL.

I would start my day with a hit of meth before the morning practice session. In the late morning or early afternoon I took a sip of my GHB-laced water bottle to relax or get some sleep before the afternoon drills. When the GHB entered my system, everything was blissful, the stress of trying to make the team was gone and The Lie was none of my concern for the next few hours. In the middle of the afternoon, I ingested some more GHB, which didn't show up in urine tests. Tara eventually discovered that I was taking GHB, but I convinced her that it was not harmful and was helping me get through the rigors of training camp. But she had no idea that I was also snorting meth.

I didn't think my substance abuse was hurting my chances to make the Saints, but there was a bigger problem: Kendall Gammon, considered one of the game's best long snappers, was still on the team's roster. Despite my skill and desire, I knew the odds of me unseating Gammon were slim.

I think part of my substance abuse back then was a way to deal with the frustration; my second tryout with the Saints was my sixth attempt to make an NFL team in less than two years, and my quest to play at football's highest level continued to be an exasperating, uphill battle. I made excuses and rationalized myself into believing the drugs were my way of letting off steam or coping with the pressures and uncertainties I faced. Sure, I told myself, I knew I indulged in meth and GHB more often than I should. And in the back of my mind I knew I had some issues. But I was still the guy who outworked everyone else. I could purge my system and work off the effects of the drugs with my daily regimen of arduous workouts and lifting sessions. If I took meth and/or GHB, I told myself that I would just work that much harder in my training session the next day … and for a while, I did. But now I was regularly using two illicit drugs.

I played in three of the Saints' four 1997 preseason games, but when the final cuts were made, I was again the odd man out.

I BECAME DISILLUSIONED and demoralized. After my release Tara and I moved to Radford, Virginia, where I worked for her dad's moving company, earning about $320 a week as I contemplated my next move. Tara initially supported my goal to play in the NFL, but she eventually became aware of my chemical dependency, and that, coupled with my inability to secure gainful employment in football, already began to take its toll on our six-month marriage. And when we learned she was pregnant around the same time I got released, the pressure grew even greater for me to find steady work.

While Tara and I were in Virginia, our marriage slowly began to crumble. It was apparent to her that I was still doing drugs; when she confronted me about it, my lame excuse was that I was slow to wean myself off some of the pharmaceuticals I had taken during training camp. But I could tell she wasn't entirely buying my story. I could also tell in her eyes that there was something about me she hadn't bargained for when we got married—something she didn't like. But I did next to nothing to make things better. Although I curtailed my meth use because I didn't have a source in Virginia, I still received a regular supply of GHB from Dale, my former Saints teammate. Tara has always been close to her parents and sister, Angie, and as The Lie grew more difficult to hide, it wasn't long before the tension between her family and me became palpable. I wanted to get the hell out of Virginia but my choices were limited.

I knew I would not be able to land a coaching job until I got my college degree, so returning to Boise State to finish school was among the options we considered.

It was around that time when I got another call from San Jose Saber-Cats general manager Terry Malley, who offered me a contract to return to the Arena Football League team for the 1998 season. I still harbored thoughts of playing in the NFL and viewed the opportunity to play in the AFL as perhaps my one last chance to showcase my talents. I agreed to Malley's offer, signed the contract he mailed me in January of '98, and told Tara we were moving to California.

I didn't ask her opinion; I just decided my football career was more important than any concerns or reservations she had. Although she still liked the idea of being married to a pro football player, she was reluctant to join me in California. She was about halfway through her pregnancy and insisted that she needed her parents' support and help when the baby arrived. "I don't give a shit," I said. "You're my wife and you're coming with me." She continued to balk and make excuses, but I refused to relent and she finally gave in a few days later. "OK, I'll tell you what," she said. "You pack up and drive out to California, and I'll fly out and join you in a couple of weeks."

In early 1998 I hauled all our belongings onto a trailer and headed for San Jose to chase my elusive dream. After I had been on the road for a few hours, I called Tara from West Virginia to see how she was doing. As we talked, I could sense something wasn't right. There was a hesitation in her voice; I was pretty sure she was waiting for the right moment to say something I wasn't ready to hear. "Tara, what's going on?" I finally asked. "Is there something you want to tell me?"

"Well … yeah," she replied. "You know … I talked with my mom and dad, and we all agree it's just not a good idea for me to join you in California right now. You know … with the baby and everything."

I hit the roof. "Well, fuck them!" I screamed into the phone. "I'm coming back to get you! Pack your stuff! Fuck you and fuck your parents! You're my wife and that's my child, too! You're coming with me!"

I turned my vehicle around right then and there. When I returned to Radford, I continued my rant and finally got Tara to acquiesce. When her parents and sister tried to intervene, Tara half-heartedly told them she was OK with the decision; given my unstable and volatile behavior, she was afraid I might do something rash or, even worse, violent, so she agreed to return to California with me. On the trip we barely spoke. It was four days of silence, cold shoulders and icy stares. And I don't blame her.

My decision to drag my pregnant wife across the country so I could play indoor football blew up in my face. The six months I spent on the SaberCats' roster in 1998 was an utter disaster—personally and professionally. My first mistake was to rent a place in Pittsburg, more than 40 miles from the SaberCats' training facilities in Santa Clara. There were dozens of towns that were closer and nicer, but I told Tara that living in my hometown would be a more comfortable fit. It was just more of The Lie. Although my decision could have been subconscious, what the move *really* did was reconnect me with my drug sources. I now had a steady supply of meth to go with the know-how and wherewithal to manufacture my own GHB. I also had a reunion of sorts with my mother and my brother Chris.

My sister, Autumn, lived with Tara and me for the first few months we were in Pittsburg, and my mom and Chris would occasionally stop by to see Autumn; in the process I reconnected with my mom (although our relationship remained somewhat strained) and she and my siblings got acquainted with Tara.

As I prepared for the '98 AFL season, I was ostensibly a professional athlete and still an NFL hopeful; I told Malley and the SaberCats that my approach to football was all about the intangibles—passion, sacrifice, work ethic. But the goals I sought seemed to be slipping away and the qualities I preached rang hollow. I had become a phony. I knew I was a drug addict. In retrospect, I knew long before the spring of 1998. Truth is,

I now believe my drug use became an addiction eight years earlier when I was a college freshman at Santa Clara. And ever since then The Lie had been tightening around me like a straightjacket.

I DID METH and GHB almost every day during those six months in northern California. I had little or no hunger and lost around 40 pounds without even trying. Before the season began, there were many occasions when the drugs coursing through my system would keep me awake for days at a time. Once the season started and I forced myself to get a few hours of sleep, I would wake up around 5:30 a.m., sip a capful of GHB, and wait for the drug's comforting buzz. Then, before I left the house around 6 a.m. for my commute to Santa Clara, I'd counter the warm and soothing effect of the GHB with a jolt of meth. Once I reached the Saber-Cats' training facilities, I would add some GHB to my water bottle every four hours or so to maintain the high I started that morning. It was a vicious circle that was almost certain to end up tragically; how I managed to drive back and forth between home and work without getting into a wreck is beyond me.

When I got home in the evening I sipped more GHB and snorted some meth behind Tara's back. At night when I was by myself The Lie filled me with guilt and remorse. I was never so miserable in my life. I felt like I was about to crash and burn. My marriage was in serious trouble and my playing career was heading for an unfulfilling end. My solution? I increased my use of meth and GHB to self-medicate.

A few weeks before training camp began I was at home doing my usual mixture when I began hallucinating. I had been awake for days and my mind was playing tricks on me. Tara was somewhere in the house, and I recall being inside our garage. In my drug-induced delirium, I thought I was addressing a group of football players to whom my father was preparing to speak; at the same time my dad was holding a pen and writing phrases on the wall of the garage. "You guys sit down and listen to him!" I shouted at the imaginary players. "Can't you see he's writing something?!"

Tara heard my yelling, entered the garage, and found me babbling and totally disoriented. She called my mother, Autumn and Chris, all of whom lived within an hour of Pittsburg. "Something's wrong with Joe," she told them. "He's on some kind of drug and he's really tripping. Please help me."

My mother and siblings arrived as quickly as they could and helped Tara get me from the garage into the house. "What's the matter with you, Joe?" Autumn asked me. I was talking incoherently and nothing I said made sense. They thought they had me settled down when I bolted out of the house and started knocking on the front doors and windows of a few neighboring houses. I was totally freaking out when my family decided to call the cops, who then called the paramedics. They got me under control and transported me to a hospital in nearby Martinez.

I was strapped to a chair with an IV stuck in my arm. When I woke up several hours later, I was in a padded room wearing only my underwear. I was released the next day after I spoke to a counselor and assured him I had regained my senses. By this time, the drug use I thought I always had under control had control of me. About a week or two later I had a similar psychotic episode while mixing meth and GHB; again Tara, about seven months pregnant at the time, called the paramedics. Again, I was taken by ambulance to Martinez, stripped down to my underwear, and placed in a padded room. This time I was designated as a 5150—a person deemed by California law to have a mental disorder requiring hospitalization. Again, I was released a day or so later, but this time it was my mother and sister who picked me up. "Where's Tara? I asked.

"She couldn't take it anymore," my mother said. "Your drug use was too much for her. While you were in the psych ward, she went back to Virginia at her parents' urging."

I had reached the end of my rope. My playing career was all but over. My wife had left me. My father was gone. I had alienated my mother and siblings. I rarely spoke to my uncle and grandmother. I wasn't suicidal; there was never a point where I thought about sticking a gun to my head. But there were times when I honestly didn't care if I saw the sun the next day. I had thoughts like, "Hey, if I take too many drugs this time they might kill me. So what? Why the fuck not?" I started to experience feelings of self-pity and paranoia. It seemed like everyone was against me.

Finally, I started to feel a little better and tried to reconcile with Tara. I was on the phone every day, begging her to come back to California. "I'm done with the drugs," I said. "I'm sorry for what I've put you through." But it was The Lie talking; I was just telling her what she wanted to hear. At first she wouldn't budge, but I finally convinced her I was sincere. "Listen," she said, "if I come back, I don't want to live in Pittsburg; you have too many bad influences there." I agreed to Tara's terms; a week or so later she rejoined me and we moved into a house in Pleasanton, 23 miles closer to the SaberCats' training facilities.

SOON AFTER THE SaberCats' season began I suffered a back injury and spent a good portion of the year on the injured reserve list. My ambition to play in the NFL had become nothing more than one maddening setback after another. I had lost my edge and I wasn't the same player I had been just a year earlier when I was at the top of my game with the Saints. My guilt was compounded because of my relationship with Terry Malley, who, as both my head coach at Santa Clara and San Jose's GM, had always been one of my most ardent supporters. Twice he had signed me to an AFL contract with scant return on his investment.

Worse yet, I failed to keep my word to Tara. Once I was placed on IR it became easy to resume my heavy use of GHB. While the team practiced and went through conditioning drills, I remained in the training area with the other injured players and team trainers, able to easily ingest the GHB I brought along in my water bottle as I did my rehabbing and physical therapy. And when I was home I didn't need to be overly surreptitious with my drug use either; by this time Tara realized I wasn't clean and sober and pretty much gave me a wide berth.

One day in the middle of the fourth week of the season, I left Pleasanton at around 6 a.m. and made my regular—and drug-addled—commute to Santa Clara. Around 8 a.m. I was lying half asleep on a training table and, like most days on IR, was high on GHB when a team trainer woke me from my blissful buzz and told me I had a phone call. "It's your wife," he said. "She needs to talk to you right away."

I got up off the table and did my best not to appear unsteady as I walked to a nearby telephone. Tara informed me that her water broke and she needed me to come get her and take her to the hospital in Walnut Creek. I acted sober enough to get dressed, tell Malley and assistant coach Darren Arbet that my wife was going into labor and I needed to leave. But before I departed the training facility and got in my car, I poured another capful of GHB into my water bottle to steady my nerves.

After I had driven about 10 minutes I was completely lost. I had lived in northern California all my life and knew the area like the back of my hand. But I was so messed up that I became disoriented and actually drove in the wrong direction. Instead of going directly from Santa Clara to Pleasanton, I took a wrong turn and ended up on the wrong highway in San Jose. Then I got stopped by the San Jose police. "I pulled you over because you were swerving," the cop said. Again, I was able to act straight enough to get off the hook. "Sorry, officer," I replied. "My wife is having a baby; I guess I'm hyped up. I'm racing home to take her to the hospital; in my haste my driving was erratic." He let me go with a warning, but I was still lost—and then I ran out of gas.

I called Tara and told her she needed to come get me. There were a few seconds of silence on the line. "You're kidding, right?" she finally said. "What the hell are you doing? You should have been here by now."

"Yeah, I know," I replied. "I got disoriented, and then I got pulled over by a cop in San Jose. Sorry."

"Why did you get stopped and what are you doing in San Jose?"

"Listen, we can talk about that later. Right now, you need to come get me so we can get you to the hospital."

It should have been a simple matter of driving about 45 minutes from Santa Clara to Pleasanton, picking up Tara, and taking her to the hospital. Instead, an hour and a half passed between the time Tara first called me and when she reached me on the highway roadside in San Jose. She was understandably upset, but she was in the early stages of labor and wasn't about to dwell on the issue of my irresponsible behavior. We got gasoline for my car and I followed her to the hospital, nearly 50 miles away.

I was there when our daughter, Haley Hope O'Brien, was born a few hours later, but I was in a drug-induced haze the entire time. I vaguely remember holding my newborn daughter in my arms a few moments after her delivery, but the day of her birth is mostly a blur.

I have done some thoughtless and ill-advised things in my life that I'm not proud of—regretful transgressions of judgment that I still find hard to forgive and forget. For the most part, however, I have reconciled my past indiscretions and have tried to be a better person and a good father. But I still struggle coming to terms with what I did the day my daughter was born. For most of us, the day we first become parents is a memorable occasion filled with happiness and joy. But I look back on May 20, 1998, with shame and embarrassment. It still haunts me that I was more of a burned-out dope fiend than a proud new dad that day.

BUT AT THE time I didn't care. I didn't care about anything or anybody except myself. I was completely selfish. I continued to blame my unhappy marriage, my unsuccessful football career, my dead father, and all my other problems on situations and circumstances other than where the accountability clearly belonged: on me. Tara didn't say anything until we came home from the hospital with Haley a day or so later. When we got settled in, she again begged me to stop taking the drugs that were ruining our life together, or what remained of it. A week or so later she said, "Look, you're at work all day. I've got a newborn and I need my mom to help me. When the season ends I want to go back to Virginia to be with my family."

I was totally against it, but given the crap I had pulled, I didn't have much of an argument. We initially agreed to go back east when the season ended in August, but when I continued my drug use Tara informed me a week or so later that she had had enough. "I'm not staying here until August," she said. "I can't do it. You can pack our stuff and join us when the season ends." I knew I was making a royal mess of everything and she had plenty of good reasons to leave. In June Tara and our month-old daughter moved to Virginia.

The SaberCats finished 7-7 and lost in the quarterfinals of the AFL playoffs in August; as soon as the season ended I packed our 1997 Ford

Expedition and a trailer and pulled it across the country to Virginia. Tara and Haley were in an apartment near her parents' home in Radford.

I unpacked everything and told Tara my drug abuse was under control; I announced that I was resolved to making amends—saving our marriage and raising our daughter together. "Everything is going to be fine," I tried to reassure her. "I'm done with the drugs."

But it was just more of The Lie.

Moreover, Tara's family wasn't buying my story. The dynamics between us remained highly volatile, and I had a heated exchange with Tara's dad and sister just hours after my arrival. They had made it clear I wasn't welcome, and now they had my recent hospitalization as proof of my chemical dependency. Although I claimed I had cleaned up my act, my entreaties for another chance fell on unsympathetic ears, and Tara had visibly grown weary of the strife and conflict my presence was causing. After I had been in Radford for less than two days she decided our situation was beyond repair. "You need to leave," she said. "This isn't working."

I think her plan was to get all her belongings back and then kick me out; I don't blame her one bit. With the deck stacked against me, I decided any further discord would be foolish and useless. I left all our belongings—everything I owned except the 1972 Cadillac Coupe de Ville I still had in California—in the apartment in Radford with Tara and flew back to the West Coast the next day.

Tara filed for divorce soon after my departure from Virginia. My life was in disarray. My marriage was over, my playing career was over, I had little money and even fewer options. I was mired in misery; The Lie had taken me to the brink of the abyss.

When I returned to California I briefly stayed with a friend in Concord as I contemplated what to do next. "So," I muttered to myself, "this is what it's like to hit rock bottom."

CHAPTER
7

IN ADDITION TO A 26-YEAR-OLD CADILLAC, the only other worldly possessions I had were a box of tools in the trunk and a duffel bag stuffed with clothes in the car's back seat. As I sulked, blamed others, and cursed my misfortune while in Concord I eventually contemplated my future and came to terms with the dissolution of my marriage and the end of my playing days. The next logical steps were to—yet again—get my act together, return to Boise State to earn a bachelor's degree, and embark on the coaching career I had long envisioned.

A number of obstacles, however, stood in my way: It was after Labor Day and the fall 1998 semester was already well under way. Also, given my decision three years earlier to drop out and still accept my athletic scholarship money from BSU, I had doubts whether I would be welcomed back into the Bronco fold with open arms—even though technically I still had scholarship funding remaining. I also worried that athletic director Gene Bleymaier and others had finally figured out that I had started the fracas at the end of the 1995 Idaho State-BSU game—and as a member of the coaching staff, no less. In addition, I was really low on cash and didn't know how I could possibly afford the 37 credit hours I needed to complete the requirements for my sociology degree. Worst of all, I remained heavily into methamphetamine and GHB. Before I departed for Boise I scored a bunch of meth.

When I showed up at the Broncos' Varsity Center a few days later and inquired about returning to school, no one mentioned my past transgressions. I decided to push my luck and asked to see Bleymaier.

"Gene, I need your help," I said as I took a seat in his office. "I've had some bad luck. My playing career is over and I don't have much money; I need to get back into school this semester. The university still owes me the last year of my scholarship."

Appearing reluctant to help, Bleymaier finally relented and suggested I re-enroll as a part-time student. But that status, he pointed out, would mean I could sign up for no more than eight credit hours that fall.

"But I need to take 37 credit hours between this semester and next spring so I can graduate in May," I said.

"Well, I can't help you then," Bleymaier responded. "You're already late as it is."

"Then what do I need to do to make this happen?"

"You'll need a presidential override."

"OK, that's what I'll do. I'm going to call [then-BSU president Charles] Ruch as soon as I leave here. I don't care what you say. I need to get this done."

Challenged by my insistence, Bleymaier became agitated. "Go ahead," he replied, "it won't do you any good; it's not going to happen."

I didn't call Ruch, and I don't know what happened after I left Bleymaier's office, but the next day I was contacted by the university and told I had been accepted on probationary enrollment status. In addition, I was still eligible for my scholarship through the athletic department's degree-completion program, as long as I met the minimum academic requirements. Moreover, despite my late arrival I was granted full-time status; I hastily made some connections with people I knew on campus and signed up for 20 hours of credits.

I was fortunate to get all the classes and the funding I needed. But I didn't fare as well with my living arrangements. Not bothering to make any housing provisions before arriving in Boise, I just assumed I could find a place to crash for a week or two until I found my own digs. After all, I figured, I had several friends and former teammates who would be glad to help me out. I figured wrong.

I quickly discovered I didn't have as many friends in Boise as I thought. Even though I was only three years removed from direct affiliation with the Broncos as an assistant coach, most of the guys with whom I played and coached were gone: Pokey Allen had passed away, his coaching staff was sent packing after the 1996 season, and the majority of those players whom I knew well had completed their eligibility and moved on. Brian Smith, for example, was playing in a pro football league in Germany at the time. In addition, the football program was in a serious state of flux. From November 1996 to December 1997 BSU had four head coaches—the dying Allen and interim coach Tom Mason during the '96 season; Houston Nutt, named to replace Pokey in December of that year; and Dirk Koetter, hired after the '97 season when Nutt bolted for the head coaching job at Arkansas. Furthermore, the Broncos were in the early stages of a difficult transition from Division 1-AA to Division 1-A football.

The Boise State football team had endured more than its share of major challenges and bad luck between the diagnosis of Allen's terminal illness in December of 1994 and Koetter's arrival three years later. And Koetter, an Idaho native and former Idaho State quarterback with an appreciation for the Broncos' storied program, did a masterful job righting Boise State's listing ship before accepting the head coaching position at Arizona State in 2000. Nevertheless, the achievements of the 1994 team and the glory it brought to Boise State seemed like ancient history and of little consequence to most of those in the 1998 program.

During my first weeks in Boise I was able to stay with a few acquaintances for a day or two, but their hospitality was short-lived. I began to fret. Perhaps I had finally blown my cover. Could The Lie, which I had managed to keep my deep, dark secret since I was a teenager, be catching up with me? Perhaps rumors of my substance abuse and my brushes with the law had finally become known to those familiar with the Boise State football program. I grew paranoid and reclusive at the thought of being exposed as a junkie. My mind was jumbled. I steered clear of the Broncos' football facilities and maintained a low profile while on campus to attend classes or study in the library. I grew frustrated and embarrassed by my meager and itinerant existence and eventually stopped asking around for places to stay.

I ended up sleeping in my car on and off that fall, sometimes for two or three days at a time. A couple of cold nights I pulled extra clothes out of my duffel bag to ward off the chill. "Man, I was an All-American at this place four years ago," I said to myself. "Now I'm sleeping in my car. How much lower can I go? Can I do this? Can I really get my degree living like this?" But I knew part of my bleak circumstances was because of my continued drug use; typical of many addicts, I sacrificed adequate food and shelter at times to maintain my meth habit and to manufacture my GHB.

Despite those moments of self-doubt and self-inflicted hardships, I remained resolute about my coaching aspirations. In spite of my misbegotten situation and personal struggles at night, I still managed to keep up appearances, remain highly functional, and plug away at my classes by day. I stayed on schedule to get my degree and took the necessary steps to stay sober enough to get my schoolwork done. Despite The Lie—with all its physiological, emotional and psychological damage—I still had the vibrant look and build of a football player. I firmly believed I would eventually overcome my personal demons and become a football coach—and a damn good one. I turned 26 that November, and even though I had been regularly ingesting methamphetamine for more than 10 years, the haggard, strung-out addict depicted in the anti-meth television commercials had yet to stare back at me when I looked in the mirror. I convinced myself much of the time that I was still the real Joe O'Brien—the Joe O'Brien whose name was linked to BSU football.

UNFORTUNATELY, THE SELF-indulgent Joe O'Brien was always just a snort of meth or a swallow of GHB away. In late October three former Boise State teammates and I decided to drive to Reno to catch the BSU-Nevada football game. My plan was to meet them 30 miles down the road in nearby Caldwell, Idaho, on Friday evening and party hearty on the way down to Reno. On Saturday we would do some gambling, attend the game, and party afterward before returning to Boise on Sunday. As I got ready to leave for the short drive from Boise to Caldwell, I decided to get a head start on the partying and took a hit of GHB. Then I did a really stupid thing: I decided to take my entire stash of GHB—four one-gallon bottles—with me. One or two smaller, inconspicuous containers would have done the trick for the two-day trip, but for some strange reason I felt the need to take all of it with me.

When I arrived in Caldwell, our group decided to let one of the guys (I'll call him Ken) drive since he had a roomy SUV. Ken and the other two guys had already been drinking and smoking weed. As we prepared to depart for Reno, I took one of the gallon bottles out of my car and placed it in the back of Ken's vehicle with the other luggage.

Ken looked at me suspiciously. "What are you doing?" he asked.

"Nothing," I replied. "What are you talking about?"

"You can't take that in the car."

"Yeah I can."

"Fuck you! You ain't taking that shit in my car!"

"OK, tell you what," I said with an edge to my voice. "You empty your bags of weed then. Empty the cocaine you've got in your pocket. What's the difference?"

"The difference is it's my fucking car!"

Our argument continued for another minute or two, but we eventually calmed down and got in the SUV. After we got on the road—and more liquor and drugs were consumed—Ken and I began to jaw at each other again. About an hour later our disagreement became more heated, and more expletives and a number of threats were exchanged. I told Ken to pull over and let me out. He and the others told me to chill, but I had had enough. "Joe, we're in the middle of nowhere," one of the others said. "You can't get out here."

"Pull the fuck over!" I yelled. "I'm fuckin' out of here!" Ken slowed to a stop. I got out, grabbed my duffel bag and gallon of "water," and off they drove to Reno.

High on GHB and stranded somewhere on Highway 95 in desolate southwest Idaho near the Oregon border, I called a fellow drug user in Boise, who picked me up around 11 p.m. As we drove back to Caldwell to get my car, I took another hit of GHB. An hour later when I got behind the wheel of my Cadillac I was totally wasted. Swerving and weaving on Interstate 84, I got pulled over by a Boise police cruiser. I agreed to take a breathalyzer because I was high on hard-to-detect GHB, not alcohol. But when the cop looked in the back of the car and saw the four gallon containers, I thought, "Holy shit, I'm busted!" Much to my relief and amazement, he didn't say anything, not realizing they were more than just jugs of water. When the breathalyzer indicated I didn't have alcohol in my system, I was able to convince the cop I was just fatigued, not drunk, and he let me go with just a warning.

Around the same time I finally got a break with my living situation when Don Copple, a Boise attorney and BSU athletics supporter, hired me to take care of some rental property he owned. Part of my payment was free rent in one of his apartments. Like everyone else who thought they knew me, Copple was unaware of my drug problem. "I didn't have a clue. Joe was a friend," said Copple about his decision to help me. "I always liked him."

Although I didn't spend a lot of time building and fixing things when I was growing up, I inherited some of my late father's manual skills, which served me well while I was in Copple's employ. From late 1998 through the summer of '99, I managed Copple's buildings—mowing lawns and performing electrical, plumbing and carpentry work, among other tasks.

Despite Copple's generosity, I was still barely making ends meet, which was part of the reason I sold some of my meth. People who use illicit drugs invariably find other users, and I was no exception. I became acquainted with two men in need of a meth source. So I started selling some of my "crank" to the pair. It was the only time I ever sold drugs directly.

That spring I spoke to Northern Arizona head football coach Jerome Souers about a graduate assistantship on his staff. Our paths first crossed in 1994 when Souers was the defensive coordinator at Montana and I played defensive end for Boise State. In a memorable game in Bronco Stadium that fall, the Broncos routed the top-ranked Grizzlies 38-14 and made life absolutely miserable for Dave Dickenson, their All-American quarterback. Our defense was relentless that day, and I had an especially good game as we recorded 13 quarterback sacks for minus-98 yards and knocked Dickenson out of the game in the second half with a severe ankle injury.

"I didn't even know Joe then, but I could tell by the way he played that he was somebody special," Souers said years later. "He played with such passion. I remember watching number 14 on BSU's defense during that game in 1994. He destroyed us. It was hard to watch, but his performance also captivated me."

It also helped that I had connections with Souers' staff at the time: Former Boise State coaches Dave Stromswold and Scott Criner, both of whom coached under Pokey Allen, were assistants with the Lumberjacks. Criner's uncle is ex-BSU coach Jim Criner, who was my coach when I played for the Scottish Claymores in 1996. Also, Scott's dad is Herb Criner, a former assistant athletic director at BSU with whom I have always had a good relationship. In addition, Souers contacted Al Borges, Pokey's offensive coordinator at Portland State and BSU and the offensive coordinator at UCLA at the time, who gave me a strong endorsement. After a couple of weeks of negotiations over the phone I received an offer from Souers, contingent on my graduation from BSU that May, to join his staff as a graduate assistant coach with the defensive line.

It was a hire that Souers took seriously. "At many of the big schools, lots of their GAs are not much more than observers, just standing around practice holding a clipboard," he said. "But at Northern Arizona and other schools at the FCS [Football Championship Subdivision] level, GAs play an important role. For us, they are often the ninth or 10th guys on our staff. They are actually *coaching*, cutting their professional teeth and developing their expertise. So when you hire a GA at our level, there is a certain element of risk. But I didn't consider it much of a risk when I hired Joe. I loved him as a player at Boise State; he played with passion, and when he joined our staff he coached the same way he played."

Finally, things appeared to be falling into place: I was just a month or so away from getting my degree, I would soon be on my way to Flagstaff, Arizona, where I was relatively unknown, and I would clean up my act— yet again—and get started on a long, rewarding and successful coaching career.

IN MAY 1999 my friends Jerry and Rosanne Haflich along with their daughter (and my goddaughter), Whitney, as well my grandmother, Minda O'Brien, traveled from California to attend Boise State's commencement ceremonies. I had not seen my year-old daughter, Haley, since the previous fall when she was less than four months old, and I missed her terribly. Whatever problems my ex-wife Tara and I had, they did not change my love for our daughter. I convinced Tara that my graduation was a good reason for me to see Haley, and she agreed to bring her to Boise.

Unfortunately, Tara's visit wasn't without incident. To begin with, her dad, with whom I never got along, accompanied her to Boise because they were concerned that tempers might flare and cause problems when Tara and I got together. They were right.

The day of my graduation Tara stopped by my apartment with Haley so I could spend some time with her before she and her mother returned to Virginia. After Haley fell asleep, it wasn't long before Tara and I began to argue. Tara said she needed to get going, and I said I wanted to keep Haley for a couple of hours. A few minutes later when Tara went out to her car to get her purse, I slammed the front door behind her.

"What are you doing?!" she yelled through the door.

"I'm keeping Haley for two hours," I answered.

"But I need to get going."

"Too bad. You've been out of the apartment for one minute; come back in an hour and 59 minutes."

"I want her *now*!"

"Tough shit!" I replied.

The commotion brought my grandmother, who was staying with me for the weekend, into the living room. "Joe, what's going on?" she asked.

"Don't worry, Grandma," I replied. "Tara and I just had a little disagreement over how long I can have Haley."

Then the doorbell rang. "Joe," Tara yelled through the door, "give me Haley *now* or I'm going to call the cops!"

"I don't give a fuck what you do!" I yelled back. "I told you to come back in an hour and 59 minutes!"

"Joe," my grandmother said, "please don't swear like that. And I can't take all this yelling."

"Listen, Grandma," I said, "this is between Tara and me. If you don't like what you're hearing, go back to your bedroom."

I could hear Tara crying. Then she banged on the door. "I'm calling the cops!" she threatened.

"Fine! Go ahead! See if I give a fuck!"

"Joe," my grandmother pleaded, "please stop!"

"Grandma, I'm sorry. But I'm not giving Haley back to her after she's been here such a short time. Can't you see it's not fair?"

"Why are you doing this?" Tara cried through the door.

I turned from my grandmother and yelled back through the door. "Because Haley is my daughter, too!" I yelled. "I don't know when I'm going to see her again, and you're taking her from me!"

When the police arrived, I refused to let them in. "Mr. O'Brien, you need to cooperate," one of the cops said.

"Sorry, I'm not doing it," I answered. "I'm with my daughter. She's safe. She's with my grandmother, and I'm within my rights to spend time with her."

I could hear Tara crying and talking to the cops. "Mr. O'Brien," the policeman said, "if you don't open the door and give us the child, we're going to have to call child services; we'll take her away by force if we have to. You and your ex-wife will then have all kinds of problems and hassles getting her back. Is that what you want?"

I was furious. I felt I had no rights as a parent. But after a few minutes I finally relented. I walked to the bedroom where Haley was sleeping, picked her up, kissed her on the cheek, held her tightly in my arms as I walked to the front door, and reluctantly handed her to one of the cops.

He gave Haley to Tara, who was still carrying on like our daughter was in some kind of danger.

"How can you do this to me?" Tara sobbed. "How could you keep me away from my baby?"

"Hey, goddamn it, now you know how I feel," I shot back.

NOT LONG BEFORE I moved to Flagstaff, I became involved with a woman named Melissa Strain, who, along with her two young daughters, was shacked up with some guy in a house across the street from Copple's apartments. I had a pretty good hunch from the telltale signs—the unkempt yard, the suspicious-looking visitors, the nocturnal noise and activity—that they were drug users. I also noticed that the guy (I'll call him Mitch) would often be gone for several days at a time. One afternoon during one of Mitch's many extended absences, Melissa and I struck up a conversation. She said she was unemployed and on welfare, and Mitch had offered her and her girls, a six-year-old and an infant, a place to stay. But once they moved in, she realized she had made a mistake. He was possessive, abusive and had a real mean streak. Her description of Mitch made my mind drift back some 17 years to Rapid City, South Dakota, when my siblings and I were subjected to the cruelties of our mom's live-in boyfriend, Brent.

"God, I'm sorry to hear that," I said. "I wish there was something I could do to help. But I'm moving to Arizona soon." But then I found out Melissa was a meth user, and despite my initial intent to keep my distance, it wasn't long before we started to hang out and do drugs together when Mitch was gone; our relationship eventually became close. Moreover, I grew quite fond of the two girls, who were sweet and loveable.

One night when Mitch was gone Melissa came over to my place. She had just put her girls to bed and brought along a baby monitor in case the little one woke up. We were sitting in my living room getting high when the baby began to cry. Melissa hurried across the street, assuming it was just a matter of a wet diaper. "I'll be right back," she said. To her surprise, an angry and inebriated Mitch was lying in wait in the child's room.

He began shouting and cursing, all of it coming loud and clear over the monitor: "YOU FUCKING WHORE, YOU SLUTTY BITCH!" he screamed. "I KNOW YOU'RE WITH THAT EX-FOOTBALL PLAYER DOING DOPE! YOU'RE SLEEPING WITH HIM, AREN'T YOU?!"

My first impulse was to rush to Melissa's aid. But as the commotion continued, I had second thoughts: "Boy, the last thing I need is to get involved in some domestic quarrel," I said to myself. "I can't afford to get in the middle of this. If the cops show up, they might start asking questions. I could get busted for drug possession; that could mess up everything and could cost me my new job." But then it sounded like Mitch was going too far: "I'M GOING TO BEAT YOUR ASS!" I heard him yell. "I'LL TEACH YOU TO FUCK WITH ME!" Melissa began screaming, and then I heard the baby crying and the six-year-old bawling.

I knew I had no choice as I raced across the street and into the house. I burst into the baby's room and proceeded to beat the living shit out of Mitch. I grabbed the dazed and bleeding Mitch by his hair and pointed my finger in his face. "You son of a bitch," I yelled. "If you even look across the street I'll beat your ass again. If I see you anywhere near them again, I'll kill you." I grabbed the two girls and told Melissa to follow me back to my place.

AFTER I RESCUED Melissa and her daughters from Mitch, they had nowhere to go and remained with me. When the time came for me to leave for Northern Arizona, they were still without a place to stay. It wasn't my intent to bring them along when I left Boise; from my perspective we were together by default. But given Melissa's indigence I felt I couldn't abandon the girls, and against my better judgment I took them with me to NAU. The four of us moved into a mobile home about 12 miles from campus.

In addition to my meth habit of a dozen years, I had been regularly using GHB for two years. But soon after I moved to Flagstaff I could no longer procure one of the ingredients needed to make the drug, and my stash of GHB soon ran out. And when my system was suddenly deprived of the chemical mixture, it triggered one of the most unbearable and excruciating experiences in my life. For the next week and a half my body's craving for GHB created withdrawal symptoms that were as sickening and mind-altering as the drug overdoses I endured a year and a half earlier in California.

My system's withdrawal from the drug put me through a living hell that I wouldn't wish on my worst enemy: shakes, cold sweats, anxiety, an irregular heartbeat, hallucinations, loss of appetite, insomnia and nausea, among other disorders. The physical ordeal of going cold turkey was worse than I could have imagined. It made my skin crawl, and the hair on my arms felt like tiny needles that ceaselessly pricked my skin. I was home on the first day of withdrawal when my heart started to pound and flutter. I began to panic, thinking I was on the verge of some kind of cardiac arrest. I walked outside of the mobile home and gazed at the sky. My senses were intensified; I felt like I was losing my mind. Melissa heard me babbling and joined me outside.

"What's the problem?" she asked. "Are you OK?"

I pointed to the clouds above, transfixed by what I thought I saw. "Look," I said, "do you see that?"

"See what?"

"Those clouds. Look. They're in the shape of a gun."

"What are you talking about? I don't see any clouds that look like a gun."

"It's a message from my dad. He's telling me that I need to get rid of my .357 Magnum before I do something stupid with it."

"Huh?"

"Listen, I want you to take my gun to a pawnshop tomorrow and sell it."

"OK," she said with a shrug. "Whatever you say."

The next morning I somehow managed to drive to work, but I was a mess. I hadn't slept in three or four days, and I was unable to concentrate or think clearly. I tried to watch some game film, but my mind was racing, and then my heart began to flutter again—as if it were about to burst from my chest. I went to Souers. Obviously, I couldn't tell him the real reason for my illness. "Coach, I'm not feeling well," I said. "I haven't felt good for a couple of days. I think I've got some kind of heart problem."

Souers put his hand on my chest. "Jeez, your heart's racing like crazy," he said. "You need to get that checked right away. Get yourself to a hospital now. I'll pay for your visit. You're excused from work and practice until you do. Do you need a ride?"

I told Souers I was able to drive, got into my car, and went to a nearby minor emergency clinic. All I wanted was something to help me sleep. I figured that if I could get some shuteye, even for just a few hours, my body would start to recover from the ravages of the withdrawal symptoms it was going through. I was honest with the attending physician and told him I was going through withdrawal from my use of GHB. "I just need some sleeping pills," I told him.

He was neither familiar with the drug nor sympathetic to my plight. "It sounds and looks like you're addicted to *something*," he said, "but I don't know what you're talking about, and I'm not going to give you a prescription under these circumstances."

"Can't you give me *something*?" I asked.

"Sorry," he replied. "What you need is a drug counselor."

I went home and missed practice that afternoon. I finally got a few hours of sleep and returned to the football offices the next day. I worried that if I missed any more time from work, Souers and the other coaches might become suspicious, so I told them that I had some heart palpitations that were now under control. But it was The Lie talking.

"I didn't know Joe was doing drugs, and the possibility that he was involved in substance abuse never entered my mind, nor was it brought up to me or anyone on my staff during Joe's tenure here," said Souers, who has been NAU's head coach since 1998.

Given our line of work—a demanding occupation fraught with many of the hidden dangers that doctors say contribute to heart disease— Souers never considered the possibility that the discomfort in my chest was drug-related.

"With the effort coaches put forth and the stress involved, it's not all that uncommon for that stress to cause heart palpitations and high blood pressure," he said. "In this profession, we work 18 hours a day, seven days a week during the season. Guys deal with the grind in different ways. Just like players, coaches have their ups and downs. I thought Joe was physically having a few bad days dealing with the stress."

I was barely eating or sleeping; I could hardly function, but I showed up for work the rest of week as our team prepared for its second contest, a road game at New Mexico. I remember next to nothing over the next few days. In fact, later that season I was watching some film from a practice session during the week when I was "sick." In the first few minutes of the video I saw myself working with the scout team, yelling instructions and holding up the signal board that gave the next play. Typically during such drills, the scout team will run 25 to 30 plays in a row with me displaying the placard. Everything looked normal. But as I watched the film, I noticed that after the first four or five plays I was no longer on the field and another coach had taken my place. To this day I don't know what happened; all I know is I never reappeared on the film during those drills or the rest of that practice session. Not wanting to call attention to my sudden and unexplained disappearance from the practice film, I never mentioned the episode to Souers or the other coaches that fall.

"I don't recall that incident, and I don't ever recall Joe being pulled from practice," Souers said more than a decade later. "But I do remember him telling me he felt ill before the team left for the New Mexico game. I told him, 'I'm sure you'll be fine; you need to make the trip.'"

My condition did not improve over the next day, but still afraid to raise any suspicions about my "illness," I made the 600-mile round trip to Albuquerque. Much like the preceding six or seven days, the trip was a blur. "I remember Joe was late for a team meal, and we had to send somebody to get him," said Souers when asked if he recalled any strange behavior on my part during that trip. "At the time he seemed disoriented and off his game. I thought he probably had some kind of flu bug; I had no idea it was drug abuse."

The next day, during Northern Arizona's 45-14 loss to the Brian Urlacher-led Lobos, I took my position on the sidelines and tried to perform my coaching duties, which included working with the special teams. But I was in a trance, basically worthless to the players and coaches who depended on me. Then I committed a major gaffe: On a third-down play with the ball in the Lumberjacks' possession, I called for the punting team to take the field. The players looked at each other in confusion, then one of the assistant coaches got in my face. "What the hell's wrong with you?!" he shouted. "It's *third* down, not fourth!"

Souers later said he assumed my poor health was the reason for my incompetence that day. "I didn't know what Joe was thinking," he said. "That was a big mistake. I think it cost us a penalty."

On the ride home I again started to hallucinate. I was sitting in back of the team bus with some players who were either sleeping or sitting quietly. But I suddenly imagined that they were passing around bottles of alcohol and celebrating like they had won the game. I was freaking out, barely able to stay in my seat and keep quiet. My mind played tricks on me throughout the night as we returned to Flagstaff.

I finally began to feel better a few days later. My appetite returned and I was able to sleep through the night. "You look a lot better," defensive line coach Kevin Peoples told me a few days later. "That thing with your heart was kind of scary. You looked terrible. You must be getting more sleep or eating better or something."

"Yeah," I said, "I'm not sure what it was. My heart was acting kinda strange, but it seems to be OK now."

In a matter of a few days, my complete withdrawal from GHB brought not only a great sense of physical and psychological relief, but also a renewed enthusiasm and energy for my job and life in general. Once I started feeling better I started coaching better. After the New Mexico game, the Northern Arizona football team also turned things around. The Lumberjacks won seven of their next nine games, including five straight in Big Sky Conference play, finished the regular season 8-3, and qualified for the Division 1-AA playoffs before losing 72-29 to eventual national champ Georgia Southern in the first round. Unfortunately, NAU later had to forfeit six games because of an ineligible player. Without the penalty, it would have been the second-most successful football season at Northern Arizona in more than 20 years.

I NEVER USED GHB again, and with my meager GA's salary of $400 a month I couldn't afford to buy methamphetamine except for a few occasions during my five months in Flagstaff. Although I drank and smoked marijuana on a regular basis during my stint at NAU, my drug dependence was at its lowest during those five months. I felt healthy and I was enjoying my job.

But my domestic situation was another matter. The main reason Melissa and I stayed together was because of my affection for her two daughters and my concern for their well-being. During my one season at NAU Melissa attended the Lumberjacks' home football games and sat with the other coaches' wives and girlfriends, but we didn't socialize with any of them—or with anyone, for that matter.

In fact, when the season ended that December and the football team held its annual awards dinner, Souers pulled me aside just before the banquet was to begin. "Joe, you're new here, so you need to know at these events I introduce the coaches and their spouses," he explained. "I know most of the coaches' wives and girlfriends, but I don't know about your home life. Who's at the banquet with you?"

"Melissa and her two daughters," I said.

He wasn't sure whom I was talking about. "OK, as a rule I don't introduce anybody unless she's your wife or fiancé. Is she one or the other?"

"No."

"Are you guys engaged? How shall I introduce her?"

"Don't bother," I replied, "because she ain't my wife and she's not going to be."

EXCEPT FOR MY lost week and a half, my overall experience at Northern Arizona was productive and positive. I had a good relationship with Peoples and the other coaches, and I greatly appreciated the opportunity Souers gave me.

"When Joe was on my staff I watched him emerge as an outstanding coach with the energy, work ethic and passion needed to excel in our profession," Souers said. "After that stretch of time early in the season with what I was told were his heart palpitations, Joe had an excellent performance for us.

"There are lots of guys who coach, but there are not a lot who have Joe's passion for the game. He has all the things you look for in a coach. He has the ability to impart that passion to his players. I could tell he was on the fast track to coaching stardom. He is a guy who is special and unique."

But what about The Lie?

"You can talk about living a lie and you can talk about duplicity all you want," Souers responded. "But Joe didn't live a lie. You can't fake what he did as a player and a coach. What he did was real. There was nothing fake about his passion. The one season Joe was with our program was *not* a lie. People want to cast stones when a guy takes a fall like Joe did. But I prefer to look at all the things he did as a player and a team captain at Boise State and as a coach here at Northern Arizona. He put others before himself all the time. We've had a lot of talented coaches come through here; Joe stands out above a lot of them. I still consider him one of the best defensive line coaches in the country."

When he learned some of the details of my 15-year battle with substance abuse and the real reason behind my heart problems in the fall of 1999, Souers seemed more upset with himself than with me.

"I should have known, and it hurts that I didn't," he said. "It crushes me that I didn't recognize it. I love Joe O'Brien. I hope and pray he coaches again."

CHAPTER
8

WHEN MIKE KRAMER, the coach at Eastern Washington, was named Montana State's head coach at the end of the 1999 season he brought Pete Kwiatkowski with him and promoted Pete from EWU's defensive line coach to MSU's defensive coordinator.

Pete and I stayed in touch after we both left Boise State, but our correspondence was sporadic. That changed in '99, however, when I was at Northern Arizona and he was in his second year at EWU. As former colleagues and defensive line coaches at our respective Big Sky schools, we exchanged information and swapped ideas about how to defend our teams' common opponents. In fact, each week in league play that year EWU faced NAU's opponent from the previous week; because of that scheduling quirk I talked to Pete every Sunday about what worked and didn't work for our defense.

When Pete called in December of that year and offered me a job as the Bobcats' defensive line coach—with a $30,000 salary and full benefits—my response was a no-brainer. It was not only a logical step in my professional progression and development, but also an opportunity to work with Kwiatkowski, not only a good friend, but also one of the best young defensive minds in college football.

It seemed the feeling was mutual. "I hired Joe because he was a natural-born coach," said Kwiatkowski, who is currently Boise State's defensive coordinator. "In fact, he was so good I figured that someday I'd be working for him."

"Kwiatkowski lured O'Brien to Bozeman because of his passion and leadership and hard work," wrote Mike Prater of the *Idaho Statesman* in 2009. "Because of his loyalty and communication skills. Because he had no idea of O'Brien's nighttime habits."

After I accepted the job at MSU, I tried to convince Melissa that she and her two daughters would be better off remaining in Flagstaff, but she insisted on moving with me to Bozeman, Montana. Not wanting to leave the girls behind, I agreed to bring the three of them with me. "But after things get settled, you and the girls are on your own," I said. "You'll need to get a job or get welfare assistance; once you do that you'll need to move out."

We stayed together in Bozeman for about eight or nine months, and I got Melissa a job during that time. But when it became apparent she didn't have any plans to leave, I moved out instead. "OK, you've got a job. You've got a place to live. You're on your own," I said when I left. "I'll help you out when I can."

That should have been my time to make a clean break.

NOW COMPLETELY OFF GHB and using meth sparingly, I honestly thought I had my substance abuse under control—yet again—when I joined the Montana State coaching staff in early 2000. MSU was already behind in the recruiting wars when Kramer assembled his new staff in Bozeman, and time, he said, was of the essence. "You guys should recruit where you're from," Kramer said in an initial meeting. "You already know the areas and the high school coaches." Four members of the staff— Kwiatkowski, quarterbacks coach Aaron Flowers, defensive backs coach John Rushing, and me—were from California. We selected our territories within our home state, and it was decided I would cover, among other places, the East Bay region of the San Francisco Bay Area, which includes the Pittsburg area. I knew in the back of my mind that it was a really bad idea; I should have said something, but I didn't.

A few days later I was on a plane to Oakland for my first recruiting trip as a member of the Montana State University coaching staff. When I arrived in northern California, one of the first things I did was hook up with my friend (I'll call him Victor Rodriguez) in Antioch. Rodriguez had previously supplied me with methamphetamine, and against my better judgment I promptly reestablished my drug connection with him.

For the next three-plus years, my frequent recruiting trips to northern California were twofold: By day I would woo football prospects on behalf of Montana State. By night I would do meth.

When I was on the recruiting trail I worked hard; I was diligent, punctual and persuasive. Most mornings I was on the road by 6. I arrived at schools throughout the area and visited with coaches. When NCAA regulations allowed me to talk to potential recruits, I spread the gospel of college football with lively self-assuredness and regaled the young men and their parents with stories about all the wonderful experiences associated with being a college football player—the excitement, the competition, the self-discovery. I believed everything I said; when I talked to those players I was not selling them a bill of goods. I believed then (and I believe now) that football and other sports teach valuable lessons that last a lifetime. But now I realize the hypocrisy of my actions. I preached one thing and did another. It was sheer deceit, The Lie playing out in front of trusting young men and their parents over and over and over.

I traveled to the East Bay region about nine or 10 times a year while in the employ of Montana State. When I was "off duty," I would usually stay with Rodriguez and partake of his meth. On one recruiting trip I stopped in Pittsburg to visit my grandmother. "Why don't you stay here, Joe?" she asked. "Why do you always have to stay at your friend's house? I'm just a few miles away." I made up some lame excuse about having all my paperwork at the other place and not wanting to disturb her in the early-morning hours. But it was The Lie talking.

Sometime in 2000 I started taking meth back to Bozeman with me for my personal use. It was a small amount—a quarter or an eighth of an ounce—so it wasn't hard to hide. It was before the September 11 attacks, so airport security wasn't very stringent at the time. I usually put the dope in my suitcase—wrapped up in a sock that was stuffed in a shoe; sometimes I would shove it down the crotch of my pants. As my dependence increased I later had Rodriguez ship meth to me during the months when I wasn't traveling to California. After 9/11 it became risky to smuggle drugs on airplanes, so Federal Express became our primary method of transport.

No one involved with MSU athletics knew about my drug use, and for the most part I stayed on my best behavior when I was out in public. There was, however, an incident in May 2000 when a fellow assistant coach (I'll call him Willis) and I had been drinking and got into a bar fight involving an ex-Bobcat player and his girlfriend in downtown Bozeman. For reasons I don't know the ex-player hated the MSU program, and he was looking for trouble the minute he saw Willis and me that night.

The guy and his girlfriend were at a nearby table, and we started exchanging barbs. Even though it was nighttime and we were indoors Willis was wearing shades, which gave the guy all the ammo he needed. "Oh, you guys all think you're cool," he said mockingly. "You've got sunglasses on and it's midnight. Well, you guys are both a piece of shit."

As he continued with his taunts and threats, I finally said, "You say another word and I'm going to beat the shit out of you."

Sure enough, he popped Willis' glasses off his face. I dropped the guy with a punch to the face, and a melee ensued. During the fracas the guy's girlfriend jumped on top of me. I didn't want to hurt her, but she ended up falling down and cutting a finger on some glass that had been broken during the fight. From what I recall, she needed two stitches. Willis and I hurried out the back door and drove away in his car, but the cops pulled us over about two blocks from the bar. Willis got a DUI, and I was faulted for the woman's injury and got charged with misdemeanor assault. Even though the woman later admitted I did not hit her, I got a deferred sentence and paid a fine.

THE MONTANA STATE football team got off to an inauspicious start in 2000 with Mike Kramer at the helm. Kramer, now the head coach at Idaho State, and his assistants inherited a program that hadn't won the Big Sky title in 15 years and finished 3-8 the previous season under Cliff Hysell. Unfortunately, things got worse before they got better. Like many struggling programs that hire a new coaching staff, MSU suffered through a miserable first season under Kramer, going 0-11 that fall.

However, the Bobcats improved to 5-6 in 2001, and three of the defensive linemen I coached—John Taylor, Nick Morasco and Jon Montoya—earned first-team All-Big Sky honors while defensive end Adam Cordeiro was a second-team selection and earned honorable mention on one Division 1-AA All-America squad. The 2001 season set the stage for a breakout year for the Bobcats in '02 as they finished 7-6 overall, defeated archrival Montana 10-7, won a share of the Big Sky championship with a 5-2 league record, and earned a berth in the Division 1-AA playoffs. Also in 2002 Montoya was an honorable mention All-American, an honor he also earned in 2000, and a repeat first-team all-league selection while three other defensive linemen—Jason Nicastro, Ray Sebestyen and Cordeiro—made All-Big Sky second team. After the disastrous 2000 campaign, the MSU defense quickly turned things around, yielding the fewest total yards per game in the Big Sky in 2001 (358) and again in '02 (307). With the dramatic improvement in the Bobcats' football fortunes, especially on defense, my stock as a coach rose as well.

To those who followed the Montana State football program I looked like a perfect fit. When I was on the football field with my players I was in my element, and The Lie dipped below the surface. "He was a natural on the sidelines," wrote Jennifer Starks in a 2009 *Contra Costa Times* article that detailed my downfall. "Life, it seemed, couldn't be better." I was becoming a popular figure in Bozeman—due in part to my willingness to grant interviews with the local media, speak at civic functions, and make other public appearances. The self-assurance and passion that served me so well as a player began to bring me the same success and recognition as a coach. I turned 30 during the 2002 season, and my stock as a young, up-and-coming coach began to soar. With MSU on the rise and Kwiatkowski as my boss, I was in an environment that allowed me to rapidly develop and flourish. I honestly felt I was destined for coaching greatness.

ALTHOUGH I WAS no longer living with Melissa, she remained in Bozeman and we occasionally got together to share my meth. After I moved out, Melissa and her two daughters moved into a house across the street from the MSU campus, and from time to time she would stop by the football offices to see me, often to ask for money—$50 here for food, $100 there for rent, another $100 for school clothes and supplies for the girls. I would occasionally stop by Melissa's house to give her tickets to MSU games and visit the girls. But I had grown weary of her freeloading. One day I finally told her I was done giving her money and she needed to fend for herself. Soon after, she came to me with a "business proposal."

"If you can score some additional meth from your friend in California, I can sell it," she said. "You and I can still have whatever dope we want, and we can make some money at the same time. If we do this, I won't need to ask you for money anymore."

I was hesitant because I knew that Melissa's scheme could jeopardize my career. But in my absolute stupidity I agreed. Our plan was pretty simple: Using Western Union or MoneyGram we would wire additional money to Victor Rodriguez for extra methamphetamine and have it sent to Melissa. She and I would meet and skim what meth we wanted for our personal use. She would then take what remained and sell it to others. I never knew who those "others" were, and I didn't care. After she made her transactions, we would split the profit.

The demand quickly grew, and so did my dependency. "Hey, this is great. I can score some dope anytime I want," I thought. "I'll do as much as I want and just have more sent up here when I run out." The rush of selling illegal drugs became like another addiction. The average amount of a delivery was a quarter of an ounce or 14 grams, a street value of about $2,800.

By this time I had been snorting methamphetamine for about 15 years. I craved the drug as much as ever and derived great pleasure from the intense high it created. But the ecstasy was short-lived, and the psychological consequences that periodically followed me throughout my years of abuse were horrendous: severe anxiety, depression, confusion, paranoia, psychotic episodes, delusions and blackouts. While my struggles with the psychological demons were immense, to this day I still can't explain how my physical appearance escaped the ravages of meth abuse. Perhaps it was because my habit, although regular, was not a daily, full-blown addiction. Moreover, I still lifted weights and exercised regularly, which may have helped stave off the telltale signs. Amazingly, my skin did not dry up, so my face was never covered with the blemishes and cracks usually caused by meth abuse. My gums did not dry out and my teeth didn't rot. With the exception of my withdrawal symptoms from GHB a few years earlier, I didn't suffer the delusion of insects and parasites crawling under my skin, so I didn't scratch at my face or other parts of my body. Although there were times when I would go days without sleep, I somehow maintained a vigorous, healthy appearance. When I was on the job or out in public I continued to look and act like a football coach.

After the 2002 football season Butch Damberger, Montana State's assistant head coach, left the program, and Kramer named me as his replacement. My star was rising. The Lie notwithstanding, I had designs on a long and successful coaching career. Fellow coaches and other observers said I had the personality and the smarts to become a head coach at the college or pro level. Coaching stardom and lucrative contracts were just a matter of time. Around that same time I decided to have a house built in Bozeman. It was all falling into place. But there was one *big* problem: I was a drug dealer.

As the Montana State football program took major strides toward respectability and the defensive line I coached became a dominant force in the Big Sky Conference, the demand for the meth I helped to supply increased and our pipeline became busier. Melissa was selling meth almost as fast as I could score it; there were periods in 2003 when we had it shipped to Bozeman as often as twice a week. I was in some kind of denial at the time, but in the deep recesses of my mind I knew I comprehended the irony. I was living The Lie and trying to deal with the fraud I had become. "I juggled two lives with a lot of guilt and a lot pain," I told the *Idaho*

Statesman's Mike Prater years later.

Then I started dating Gracie Duffy.

A STRIKING, AUBURN-haired, blue-eyed Montana State senior from Great Falls, Gracie was also a cheerleader for the Bobcats. I was immediately attracted to her and remember watching her perform on the sidelines during MSU's football games. But since I was a coach and she was a student I was hesitant to say much more than a friendly hello when our paths crossed.

Our first physical contact actually occurred in November 2002 on the field in the middle of Washington-Grizzly Stadium in Missoula after Montana State defeated Montana 10-7 to earn a share of the 2002 Big Sky title. When the game ended, there was a celebration on the field among the Bobcat players, coaches, cheer squad and other spectators, and in the excitement Gracie came running up to me and jumped into my arms in celebration. After that I was *seriously* smitten. We later ran into each other in downtown Bozeman and had our first meaningful conversation. After that we called and e-mailed each other for a while. Our first date was on a Thursday evening a month or so before her graduation: March 27, 2003. It turned out to be one of the most important days of my life because I knew almost instantly that I was in love with her. I can't say that about anybody else. I don't truly know if I loved anybody before that.

Our relationship became serious, and that summer Gracie moved in with me. I didn't say anything to her—or to anyone—about my meth use and drug trafficking, and I certainly never used drugs around her. In fact, my use of meth was now limited to the occasional weekend when I stayed in Bozeman and she would go to Great Falls to visit her family. I knew I was risking both my career and my future with Gracie. To lessen the odds of getting busted as a drug dealer, I knew I had to stop my meth pipeline with Melissa—although I wasn't willing to quit The Lie entirely and end my personal use.

Melissa and I had lived apart for more than two years; our meth connection and my soft spot for her daughters were the only reasons I maintained my association with her. As I tried to distance myself from her and move on with my life, she grew bitter and resentful, and when Gracie entered the picture her anger escalated. One day Melissa asked me for $100 to buy her daughters some school clothes. "No, I already told you I'm not helping you anymore," I said. "You're going to have to find somebody else to help you. This is over. I bought a house. You know I'm in another relationship."

Her response was loud and livid: "Well, fuck you, mister assistant head football coach, drug-dealing, drug-using son of a bitch!"

"Whoa, whoa … calm down," I said.

"Well, *fuck you*! I'll fucking tell everybody! I don't give a shit! I know Kramer! I know Kwiatkowski! I'll tell them all, you son of a bitch! I've got nothing to lose! I'll blame it all on you! I'll blame everything on you! I'll tell them everything!"

I finally got Melissa to calm down, but it was obvious this was not the time to tell her I was going to stop our meth distribution. And now I had to deal with her threats.

IN THE EARLY summer of 2003 I told Victor Rodriguez that I was ending my involvement in our meth shipments. He had no objections and said I could still buy from him for my personal use. But he added that he would not continue the pipeline without me. I knew that would infuriate Melissa. Not only had I finally made it clear that whatever kind of personal relationship she thought we still had was over and I was with Gracie, but I also was about to inform her that her supply of meth was shutting down, which for her was a significant source of income.

When I called Melissa and told her of my decision and that Rodriguez would not deal with her, she let loose with more threats and a string of profanities. I was scared to death that she was going to seek revenge, blow the whistle on me, and expose my involvement in our criminal activity. But I stopped the meth shipments anyway.

Over the next few weeks my panic and fear worsened. Seeking some kind of help, I went to Kwiatkowski. Pete, a man of few words who is hardly known for his soft side, was working at his computer when I walked into his office.

"Man, Melissa is threatening some crazy shit and using me," I said. "I'm worried about it."

Succinct as always, Kwiatkowski responded without even looking up from his computer: "Cut her loose, man."

"Well, she's threatening me," I said, "and she's going to tell all these stupid lies about me. I'm just worried about it. ... You know what I mean?"

"Why do you keep giving her money?"

"I don't know. ... She's got me over a barrel."

"What do you mean?"

"Because ... well, never mind."

Pete continued to type; I wasn't even sure if he was listening. He seemed more interested in what was on the screen than our conversation. After several seconds of silence he finally spoke up: "You need to stay away from that chick, man. That's the last thing you need, or anybody needs."

As I prepared for my first season as Montana State's assistant head coach I did my best to help the team prepare for its Aug. 30 season opener against Wyoming, but I struggled to concentrate on the task at hand and grew paranoid at the thought of being uncovered as a drug dealer and a hypocrite. Seeking some way to put my mind at ease, I called Melissa. "Let me just meet you somewhere," I said, "and let's just talk about this."

"No! Fuck you!" she yelled into the phone. "You're just going to try and come and tell me what I want to hear. We've been down this road before. Fuck you! I'll tell them everything!"

Desperate to end the nightmare, I made a suggestion. "If I get you one more package of meth, will you leave me alone?" When she agreed, I contacted Rodriguez and told him I wanted to place one final order. It had been months since the last shipment.

ALTHOUGH MONTANA STATE opened the 2003 season with a 21-10 loss to Wyoming, the Bobcats had high hopes for another title run and returned another stellar defensive squad under Kwiatkowski. As the team prepared for its second game of the year, a non-conference contest on Sept. 6 against Gardner-Webb, I began to make arrangements for our last shipment of meth—even though I had a bad feeling about the entire deal.

I wanted to physically distance myself as much as possible from the package when it arrived in Bozeman, so I arranged to have it delivered to Melissa on Friday, Sept. 12. That particular day was at the end of a bye week for Montana State following its 38-3 win over Gardner-Webb, and I was scheduled to be in Great Falls on a recruiting and scouting trip. I was using Gracie's Ford Focus and planned to meet her there that evening and stay with her parents that weekend.

Despite my trepidation, I still expected my share of the stash. "All right, same deal," I told Melissa a day or so before the package was to arrive. "Just give me a little bit; you keep the rest and do whatever you're going to do with it. Just remember, I'm not going to do this again."

Melissa and I decided to rendezvous in Helena—about halfway between Great Falls and Bozeman—at noon Friday after she claimed the package at the Bozeman FedEx shipping center. I had recruiting visits to the two high schools in Great Falls—Great Falls High at 7:30 a.m. and C.M. Russell in the late afternoon—and was scheduled to scout a high school game that night with Kwiatkowski and Rob Christoff, MSU's linebackers coach. I figured I'd make my stop at Great Falls High, make the one-hour drive to Helena, meet Melissa and score my portion of the meth, return to Great Falls, make my afternoon appointment at CMR in plenty of time, attend the evening game with Pete and Rob at Great Falls' Memorial Stadium, and then spend a nice, relaxing weekend with Gracie and her parents.

As I got ready to leave for Helena, Melissa called. "I'm gonna be late. I ran out of gas," she said.

"What?! How the hell do you run out of gas? You don't have two dollars in your pocket to get to Helena?" I asked sarcastically.

There was a nervous tone to her voice. "Hey, you're stressing me out," she said.

"OK, call me when you're back on the road. You're screwing up my day now. This was supposed to be easy. You go an hour, I go an hour, and we're back in an hour. That's it."

"I know, I know. Sorry."

About 45 minutes later she called again. "Where are you? What's going on?" I asked with more than a hint of annoyance in my voice.

"I got gas, but you're not going to believe this. I got a flat tire," she answered. "I'm still in Bozeman."

"*What*?! Listen, I'm on my way to Helena, but I've got to get back to Great Falls this afternoon. I'll bypass Helena and meet you in Winston. You won't have to come as far."

"All right, I got the tire fixed. We'll meet there."

Meeting in Winston would save Melissa about 20 minutes of driving, but I was running out of time to make it back to Great Falls for my afternoon appointment.

The real reason for the delay was because a few hours earlier the Missouri River Drug Task Force busted Melissa as she left the FedEx center in Bozeman with a shipping envelope in her possession. It turns out our drug ring had been under police surveillance for well over a year. Somewhere down the road, some of Melissa's "customers" informed the MRDTF, the primary anti-drug law-enforcement unit in Montana, that she was their supplier. It didn't take long before I was linked to her.

When confronted by several law-enforcement officials, she was asked what was in the parcel and whose it was. "It's Joe O'Brien's," she answered.

The oversized cardboard envelope was immediately confiscated, and when half an ounce of meth was found, the cops told Melissa she had two choices: Take the blame for everything and almost certainly go to jail for drug trafficking. But if it's Joe O'Brien's, they said, then we're going to wire you up, and you're going to go deliver it to him right now.

IT WAS EARLY afternoon by now, and another 45 minutes or so passed as I drove south on Highway 287 toward Winston and waited to hear from Melissa. She finally called.

"Where the fuck are you?!" I yelled into the phone. "I could have driven back and forth to Bozeman six times by now! I've got to be back in Great Falls soon!"

"I'm still running behind," she said. "I'll meet you in Townsend. As soon as you get into town there's a gravel parking lot to the left. If I get there first, you'll see my car."

It was another 20 to 30 minutes from Winston to Townsend. I should have said, "Fuck it. Keep my portion and I'll see you later." But my meth addiction wouldn't allow me to turn around and return to Great Falls. I continued on to Townsend, arrived at the parking lot, and sat and waited. Melissa called and said she was 10 or 15 minutes away.

When her car approached, I nervously looked at my watch. "Cool. I'm good," I said to myself. "It's 2 p.m. I can be back to Great Falls in time."

Melissa pulled up; there were no other vehicles or people around. I got out, walked a few feet to her car, opened the door on the passenger's side, and got in. I tried to suppress my frustration and anxiety and forced a smile. "What's up?" I said. "Goddamn it, it took you forever to get here. What's going on?"

"Yeah," she said. She appeared unusually nervous.

"Well, where is it?" I asked.

"It's in the trunk."

"What? Why is it in the trunk?"

"'Cause I don't carry it in here, you son of a bitch!"

"What are you yelling at me for? What's going on? I'm doing you a freakin' favor, driving to Townsend. What's the problem here?"

She got out of the car, which was her signal to the cops that she was about to give me the FedEx envelope with the meth. She walked to the trunk, opened it with her key, took out the envelope, returned to her side of the car, and got back in. "Here," she said, handing me the envelope.

"What are you doing?" I asked. "I just want my share."

She didn't answer my question. Instead she just blurted out, "I'm fucking done with you!"

"What? What are you talking about?"

"Just get the fuck out of my car!"

"What? What's your problem? I don't want all this. What the fuck is the matter with you?"

She started to get emotional. "Get the fuck out of my car and I don't ever want anything to do with you again!" she yelled. "I'm leaving the state next week."

I tried to hand the envelope back to her. "This will make you the money you need to get out of here if that's really what's going on," I said. "Are you sure? Is this how it's going to be?"

She looked at me and started crying, "Yeah, it is."

As I prepared to get out of Melissa's car, she sat with her head in her hands. My mind began to race. "Well, good," I said to myself. "Good for her, and good for me. ... You know what? Whatever. This dope will last me six months, so great."

I got out, walked to Gracie's car, got behind the wheel, opened the envelope, and pulled out a small package wrapped in paper.

Then I heard a female voice; it wasn't Melissa's.

The voice said: "FREEZE!"

CHAPTER
9

THE VOICE SHOUTED A SECOND COMMAND: "Hands up! Put your hands up!" With gravel and dust flying, what seemed like a dozen unmarked police cars came roaring out of nowhere. They descended on Gracie's car in a matter of seconds as I sat behind the wheel. I immediately dropped the envelope onto my lap and raised my hands over my head.

With about 30 guns pointed at my head, the cop who had barked the orders approached the car. The revolver in her hands shook violently as she ordered me out. I sat there stunned, staring in disbelief down the barrel of her gun. She was trembling so hard I thought her weapon might go off. My mind raced: It was all over—my career, my life with Gracie, my world … everything. My next thought was, "Please, lady, shoot me. Get it over with. Pull the trigger."

It was surreal, like I was in the middle of a bad dream. My ears were buzzing as I slowly got out of the car with my hands in the air. The cops surrounded me, grabbed my arms, put me in handcuffs, and read me my rights. I just kept thinking, "This is not happening." As I stood there I glanced over at Melissa, a few yards away. She was crying as I watched her climb into her car and drive off. I never saw her again—not even in federal court several months later when we were both convicted as meth ring co-conspirators.

I was arrested for possession of crystal methamphetamine and transported to the Broadwater County Jail in Townsend.

When Mike Kramer visited me in jail that night, I immediately started lying. "Melissa said she was leaving town for good the next day and wanted to pay me back some of the money she owed me," I claimed. "She said she wanted to say goodbye and give me some money, but it was dope. She totally set me up."

Tommy White, a Bozeman attorney and Montana State athletics supporter, also visited me that night and agreed to represent me at my initial hearing; panic-stricken and desperate, I told him the same story. Given the concerns I voiced to Pete Kwiatkowski about Melissa a few weeks earlier, I thought my alibi seemed plausible. Gracie came to see me the next day; I told her the same lie.

In a matter of hours, news of my arrest and incarceration was widely reported in the media. Words that sickened and frightened me blared from a TV near my cell: "*Montana State assistant head football coach Joe O'Brien was arrested and jailed in Townsend Friday following a sting operation when an informant allegedly delivered half an ounce of crystal meth to him,*" the reporter intoned. "*The MSU athletic department announced that O'Brien has been suspended with pay pending further investigation.*" I spent a restless and tense 2½ days in jail. I was sick to my stomach. I didn't really know what to do or think. I just wanted to die.

I appeared in Broadwater County Justice Court in Townsend Monday morning and was charged with one count of possessing crystal meth and one count of intent to distribute the drug, both felonies. The half-ounce of meth in the FedEx envelope had an estimated street value between $1,400 and $1,700. Bail was set at $15,000 with another hearing in district court scheduled for later that year. I did not enter a plea and posted my bail immediately. I was out by 10 a.m. Gracie was waiting for me, and we drove back to Bozeman in awkward silence.

MY ARREST CREATED a furor within the Montana State community, and even though I remained in denial and maintained my innocence, more accusations emerged. Law-enforcement authorities suspected I was involved in drug deals and had been under surveillance "for several months," Bozeman police detective Greg Megargel, a member of the Missouri River Drug Task Force, told the media.

Then the *Bozeman Daily Chronicle* dredged up my involvement in the altercation more than three years earlier with the ex-MSU player and his girlfriend in a Bozeman bar. "This isn't the first time O'Brien has had a run-in with the law since coming to MSU," the paper reported. "In May 2000 he was charged with misdemeanor assault after police said he pushed and injured a woman." Then rumors started flying: I was selling meth to kids and/or giving it to Montana State athletes, neither of which was true. Nevertheless, the fallout was harsh and acrimonious.

"As far as I'm concerned O'Brien is a liar and a criminal; I want nothing to do with him," said one person close to the MSU athletic program. "As a coach here he befriended my son and was great to him. But now I have to wonder if he was doing that so he could sell him drugs."

"His dirty secret was now out there for everyone to see," wrote Andrew Hinkelman of the *Daily Chronicle* a few years later. "MSU's assistant head football coach was allegedly dealing in meth, at the very least. Disbelief and anger erupted from the Bobcat faithful."

Bozeman is not a big town. Although I kept a low profile, I couldn't escape the public eye. Sarcastic remarks, insults and invective were tossed my way. I was persona non grata on the MSU campus and other places in Bozeman. "O'Brien found himself on an island," Hinkelman wrote. "Friends, family and colleagues distanced themselves. Some abandoned him altogether."

Not everyone deserted me, but my detractors far outnumbered my supporters. I still had Gracie. I'm still amazed that she stuck with me, especially when things were their bleakest, and I'm forever grateful she did. She should have left my sorry ass a long time ago. She wasn't blind: She read the stories in the newspaper and heard the accusations. She heard the whispers when we were together out in public. Yet she remained by my side.

Ray and Vicky Cordeiro, the parents of Adam Cordeiro, a three-time all-conference defensive lineman who played for me at MSU, also remained supportive. "I just couldn't believe he could do that," Ray Cordeiro told the *Daily Chronicle*'s Hinkelman. "He had been so good with the kids, he had done so much for them that I just couldn't believe that he would do anything to harm them, even though it was himself that he was hurting."

Brian Smith, my friend and former Boise State teammate, was also "shocked and dumbfounded" when he learned that I had been apprehended on drug charges. "It was more disbelief than anything else," said Smith, who was a player/coach for the Tri-City Diesel, an arena football league team in Kearney, Nebraska, at the time. "I knew Joe was enjoying a fair amount of success at Montana State, and I wasn't surprised at that. He's a natural-born coach. I know Joe and what a great teammate he was and what great character he has. So when I first heard the news about his problems with the law I was numb. It was a personal setback for me because people have always gravitated toward him, and I'm one of them."

I know my arrest disappointed and dismayed a lot of people—ex-teammates like Smith; former coaches such as Joe Aliotti, Terry Malley and Jerome Souers; and friends like the Cordeiros and Jerry and Rosanne Haflich, to name a few—and I'll always be grateful to those who believed in me and expressed their support during those dark days when I was under indictment. But if there is one person who could have—and maybe should have—thrown me under the bus, it's Pete Kwiatkowski.

From the time we first met in 1993 when he was my position coach at Boise State through today, Pete has been a good friend and a valued colleague. He was upset with me after I got busted, but he always had my back—even if his words weren't always the most comforting. "At first it was a sense of shock and disbelief," he told one reporter. "Then, as the facts came out, it became a feeling of betrayal. It's not like there was this immediate sense of forgiveness."

As a longtime friend and my boss at the time of my arrest, that wasn't the first time Pete was asked to comment on my troubles and adversities. In 2009 I briefly re-entered the coaching ranks as a volunteer with the Central Valley Coyotes of the Arena Football League 2 when Brian Smith, the team's defensive coordinator, convinced head coach Fred Biletnikoff Jr. to bring me aboard. My stint with the Fresno, California, team included home-and-away games with the Boise Burn, which led to lengthy feature stories in the sports pages of the *Contra Costa Times* and the *Idaho Statesman.*

Quoted in both articles, Kwiatkowski's support remained steadfast, but he did admit that my downfall was as baffling as it was reprehensible: "I was shocked," he told the *Statesman's* Mike Prater. "I was so close to him. It was like, wow, because no one had a clue. It never affected his work, him being on time, or his production. It was one of the saddest experiences of my life."

It is still painful to recall some of Pete's comments in the *Times* when reporter Jennifer Starks asked him about his initial reaction to my arrest. "It was as if somebody knocked the wind out of you," he said. "You don't want to believe it. What in the hell could make someone do that? It was difficult to understand how he could throw all of that away."

Despite his disapproval and disappointment, Pete is one person who has gone to bat for me in both the good times and the bad: At my sentencing hearing in 2004 he spoke on my behalf in federal court; three years and eight months later on the best day of my life, he was a member of our wedding party when Gracie and I got married.

THE DAYS IMMEDIATELY following my arrest were agonizing. I met with MSU athletic director Peter Fields, then-university president Geoff Gamble, and other school officials as they conducted their investigation. I had an uneasy feeling that their minds were already made up; a week and a half later they concluded their findings and told me I had two choices: resign or be fired.

Dan Buckley, my new lawyer, advised me to resign, primarily to avoid more unfavorable publicity. I started lying to Buckley, too. I told him what I told everybody else: Bent on revenge, Melissa had set me up. But I only shared with him the parts of my story that worked to my favor, truth be damned.

"OK, we'll fight it," Buckley said. "She tried to blackmail you. But you've got to be totally honest with me. I've got to know everything if I'm going to know how to fight for you."

I looked him straight in the eye. "I'm telling you, Dan," I said. "I'm being totally honest with you." Despite the crimes I perpetrated, the years of lying and wrongdoing, and the preponderance of evidence against me, I was still lying through my teeth to stay out of jail.

Soon after I resigned from the MSU football program I got a job as a roofer in Bozeman and awaited my next court hearing. Gracie and I were living in the house I recently had built, and I needed a job to make the house payments and to keep my sanity. The stress of the impending hearing and the certainty of a criminal trial were unbearable, but calming my nerves with meth or any other illicit drug was out of the question, so I turned to alcohol to ease the tension. I started drinking heavily—as much as a fifth of vodka a day, if not more. Beer, Jack Daniels, it didn't matter. I would even down a few shots in the morning before I went to work just to cope with the tension, and I got wasted almost every night. Gracie did her best to dissuade me from my overindulgence, but I didn't listen.

As Buckley prepared my defense, he concluded that my arrest was based on illegal search and seizure of the Federal Express package containing the meth. When the police confronted Melissa on Sept. 12 and she told them the envelope in her possession was mine, they needed my permission to open it, he explained. But they didn't, Buckley asserted, thus violating Montana's search and seizure laws when they opened the parcel and found the meth. "They screwed up," he said. "They arrested an innocent man. You're probably going to get off."

I acted as if it was obvious that I had been wrongfully arrested and accused. "Hey, Dan, that's great," I enthused. I didn't tell him that I knew the parcel contained meth, not money. I didn't care about telling the truth, the specter of committing perjury, or damaging Buckley's reputation. All I could think was maybe The Lie would work its magic one more time and get me off the hook.

Six months later, in the spring of 2004 as the date for my next hearing approached, Buckley remained confident that we would receive a favorable decision. The state prosecutors might not go for a dismissal, he said. "But then we can take a plea on a lesser charge, or we can just continue to fight it by trial," he added. "We can make that decision later. Either way, I'm fairly certain that this is all going to work out."

I was elated and guardedly relieved. I allowed myself to think my sentence might be minimal, my reputation perhaps salvageable, and my relationship with Gracie made stronger. I even harbored visions of complete vindication with a triumphant return to the college or pro coaching ranks.

Several days later I got a phone call from Buckley in his office in Bozeman. "We need to meet in my office today," he said tersely.

"Can't you talk to me on the phone?" I said. "I've got work today."

"No, you need to come to my office *today*."

"OK, I'm in Big Sky on a roofing job; I can be there by 6 p.m."

"I'll be waiting."

I knew he was mad about something. I was nervous as I drove the 30 miles from Big Sky to Bozeman, wondering what was up. Buckley was alone in his office when I arrived. "Have a seat," he said. I grabbed a chair next to his desk. He looked at me and said, "You've been lying to me the whole time."

"What? What are you talking about?" I replied, trying to act surprised and offended.

Buckley wasn't interested in my indignation, nor was he buying my act anymore. "Listen, I've got good news and bad news—really bad news."

"What's that?"

"Well, the good news is the state dropped the case."

"OK, what could be bad news?"

"The federal government picked it up, and you're going to jail."

"What are you talking about?!" I said in disbelief. "I told you what happened. I told you I was set up. I told you I didn't know—"

"Stop your lying!" Buckley angrily interjected. "Don't lie to me anymore. You've been lying to me the whole time. You need to tell me what's going on here and now. Listen to me: You. Are. Going. To. Jail.

"I don't know for how long—it could be 15 years, it could be 10 years, it could be five. I don't know what it's going to be, but your ass is going to jail. The feds have taken over the case and they have a very high conviction rate."

When the state attorneys charged with my prosecution found out about Buckley's plan for a motion to get me off on a technicality, they contacted him and said no effing way. "They told me the police had been watching you for months," he said. "They told me they have all kinds of evidence against you." My attorney's anger escalated as he spoke. "They told me you are a liar," he seethed. "They don't like liars. So they've given your case to the feds.

"So, you need to start telling me the truth. Now! The best thing we can do is plea out. You better start being remorseful for the things that you've done. And you need to start telling me what it is that you've done."

Someone had finally called my bluff. Finally caught in my own web of lies, I felt a certain amount of relief and came clean to him; from that point forward I was straight with Buckley, but only Buckley. I still did not tell the whole truth to anyone else—not even Gracie.

ONE EVENING IN mid-May 2004 when Gracie was gone for a day or two, the stress of my upcoming hearing and the thought of imprisonment became too much; I scored some meth for a few hours of escape. I hadn't touched the stuff in about nine months, but once again I succumbed to the power it still had over me.

The next morning I was summoned to appear in federal court and told a preliminary hearing on my case would be the following day in Butte. With Buckley at my side I pled not guilty. It was Wednesday, May 19, eight months and one week after my arrest on meth charges in Townsend. The judge and the attorneys began discussing dates for my bail hearing when the prosecuting attorney made a motion that I be held in custody until my bail was set. Buckley immediately objected. "What are you talking about?" he said. "My client is not a flight risk. He's made every appointment we've had. He's arrived at all of our meetings on time. He's gainfully employed. Why is it necessary that he be detained? I'll take full responsibility for him."

A discussion among Buckley, the federal prosecutor and the judge ensued. The judge eventually ruled in the prosecution's favor and ordered that I be held in custody until my bail hearing two days hence in Billings. Buckley objected but was overruled. As we stood before the bench, he learned over and said to me, "You'll be out in two days, I promise you."

Just when we thought the hearing was over, the judge ordered that I have a urinalysis done before being taken into custody. "Oh shit, that's not a good idea," I muttered to myself.

"I have some urinalysis kits in my car, your honor," the prosecutor volunteered. "I'll have one of my associates go get one." Like a pregnancy test, this urinalysis provides immediate results.

"What?" Buckley blurted out a few minutes later when we were told I tested positive for methamphetamine. For a few desperate moments, The Lie kicked in yet again. "Your test is wrong," I said to the prosecutor. But I knew I was wrong—and I was busted right there in a court of law.

I had been honest with Buckley since the angry confrontation in his office, but I didn't tell him about my meth use two nights earlier. My 15 years of duplicity and deceit finally caught up to me. I had run out of excuses, alibis and options.

I could conceal The Lie no longer.

"Dan, tell the judge I don't want a bail hearing," I told Buckley. "We're not going to Billings. If I'm going to jail right now, so be it. Let's just get this over with."

CHAPTER
10

I ASSUMED MY APPEARANCE IN FEDERAL COURT in May 2004 was just another in a seemingly endless series of appeals and delays. When I arrived in Butte that morning I figured the judge would set yet another date for yet another hearing and I would return to my roofing job that afternoon, or the next day at the latest. Even when I decided to forgo my bail hearing, I presumed I would get out on bail in a day or two because of my pre-trial status.

Instead, I was handcuffed, taken into custody, and transferred to the Jefferson County Jail in nearby Boulder because the jail in Butte was full. As the ensuing hours turned into days—and the days into weeks—my mind raced and my stomach churned as I contemplated the probability that I was stuck behind bars for the long haul. During the five months I was held in the Boulder jail I struggled with a range of emotions—anger, anxiety, vengeance and self-pity—but I also attained a certain sense of relief as The Lie slowly began to fade away. I was confined to a six-foot by nine-foot cell with a bunk bed and a steady parade of cellmates—from drunks to felons to James Bischoff, the controversial Montana doctor and mercy-killing advocate who was charged with murder for his role in an elderly woman's physician-assisted suicide.

I was allowed out of my cell for an hour each day and given access to an enclosed yard that had a basketball court. My exercise options were walking around in circles or shooting baskets. In either case it was the only opportunity I got to breathe a little fresh air. I wrote letters to Gracie and talked to her on the phone almost every day. She visited me as often as she could, and Ray and/or Vicky Cordeiro also came to see me three times a week without fail. I will always be grateful to them for their unwavering support. During my incarceration I learned that Victor Rodriguez, Melissa Strain and a 20-year-old Bozeman resident named Matthew Monts, who reportedly bought and resold meth from Melissa, had been arrested and were named co-conspirators in my case.

The federal prosecutors and investigators involved in the proceedings, led by assistant U.S. attorney Joshua Van de Wetering, would periodically meet with Dan Buckley and me as they continued to build their case. Buckley did his best to defend my rights, but we all knew the feds had me by the short hairs; it was no longer a matter of *if* I was guilty, but rather the severity of my sentence. Faced with that stark reality I prayed that Buckley would somehow find a way to mitigate the harsh penalty—a maximum of 20 years in prison and a $50,000 fine—that most federal courts mete out for charges related to the distribution of methamphetamine. I hoped that those who would decide my fate would realize that I was not a miscreant or a hardened criminal, but a decent person who made a number of bad choices. I also knew the odds were against me and it was time to plea-bargain.

Assuming I was headed for more time behind bars, I based my decision on two key factors. First, I was told that I was a possible candidate for the Federal Bureau of Prisons' Residential Drug Abuse program (RDAP), which, if successfully completed, could shave months off my sentence. For that to even be considered, the lawyers advised, it would be wise for me to plea-bargain. Second, when I asked Buckley about time served, he assured me that the clock on my sentence had started with my incarceration in May.

"Are you sure?" I asked him more than once. "So if I plead guilty, whatever time I'm doing now counts toward my overall sentence?"

"Absolutely," he answered. "If you've already done six months and you're sentenced to four years in prison, you only do 3½ years."

"OK then. I don't want to be in here, and I feel powerless to do anything about it," I said, "but as long as this time counts as time served I guess I can live with that."

In July I appeared in front of U.S. district judge Donald Molloy in Helena and was charged with meth possession, conspiracy to distribute methamphetamine, distribution of meth in the vicinity of a school, and 24 counts of money laundering that totaled $13,400. I strongly disagreed with the school-related charges because I never took part in any transactions other than with Melissa Strain. However, some of her drug deals took place in her house, which was within 1,000 feet of the Montana State campus. Mindful that it was in my best interest to cooperate with the prosecution and go along with everything, I pled guilty to all charges. Molloy accepted my plea and set Oct. 15 in Missoula for my sentencing.

I WAS DESPONDENT and dispirited—especially by the thought of a lengthy separation from Gracie. I knew my confinement and the uncertainty of my fate were causing her a lot of stress. She told me her aunt had urged her to end our relationship. Of all the terrible things that were happening to me, losing Gracie, who turned 24 while I was in the Jefferson County Jail, would have been the worst. Yet I understood that it was unfair to string her along—especially if I was going to receive a lengthy prison sentence. One day when she came to see me, I looked at her through the thick glass window that separated us.

"I know you're under a lot of pressure, that you're being told our relationship has no future," I said, trying to maintain my composure. "I have a suggestion: Let's just take this in phases. Let's wait until my sentencing. Then we'll know what we're dealing with.

"If I get 10 years, then there's a problem. I love you, Gracie. I love you enough to say, 'Hey, if I'm in for 10 years, I don't think you should be waiting around for me for 8½ years or whatever. You've got to do what you've got to do.' But what if it's five years? From what other guys in jail tell me, and what Dan Buckley tells me, five years is the average sentence for a first-time, non-violent offender like me. And then I might get into a drug rehab program in prison, which could shorten my sentence even more.

"You're guaranteed six months in a halfway house if you get into the drug program, so that's six months off, too. So we're talking about major time getting out early. I've talked to guys who were sentenced to 24 months, and they're out in nine because they were eligible for and took part in the drug program. This is really what can happen. I mean, I don't know for sure and there's no guarantee I'll get in the program, but let's wait and see. Plus, whatever time I serve before my sentencing counts as time served. Then maybe I could be out in three years or less."

I must have sounded desperate or was getting overly emotional because I certainly had her attention.

"Maybe I'll get lucky and only get 36 months," I continued. "I mean, I don't know what's in store for me, but I'm just asking you to at least wait until my sentencing before you decide anything. Let's not make any hasty decisions right now. Who knows? Maybe I'll be out in 18 months."

My heart was pounding and my stomach was tied up in knots as I spoke through the window. I wanted so badly to reach out and touch her. I didn't know if my plea made my situation better or worse, but I knew I had to say *something*. I couldn't just let her go without a fight.

Gracie sat there for a moment. "You know what? That sounds like a good idea," she finally said. "What you say kind of puts things in perspective. OK, let's see what happens."

When she left I breathed a huge sigh of relief and the knot in my gut loosened just a bit.

ON FRIDAY OCT. 15, three weeks before my 32nd birthday, I was taken to federal court in Missoula to appear in front of Molloy for my day of reckoning. The anxiety was almost unbearable. How I would spend the next several months, if not years, of my life as well as my future with Gracie hung in the balance—not to mention having to endure the unabated public humiliation and stigma of being labeled a drug dealer and a convicted felon.

I wore a black suit and tried to look as calm and composed as I could; inside, though, I churned. As I walked into the courtroom I saw Gracie and her mom in the gallery. In another row sat Montana State coaches Rob Christoff and Pete Kwiatkowski, as well as Vicky Cordeiro and Jerry Haflich, among others. It had been 13 months since my arrest in Townsend. Based on my guilty plea in his court three months earlier, Molloy was about to sentence me on three federal drug charges and 24 counts of money laundering. But before he rendered his decision Kwiatkowski, Cordeiro and Haflich spoke on my behalf. Their statements were all along the same lines.

"Joe O'Brien is one of the best coaches I have ever been around," Kwiatkowski stated. "He's like a brother to me. He'd give you the shirt off his back if you asked him. When he was on the job, he always acted in a professional manner. He was great with the kids. In fact, he had players swarming to his office all the time, asking for help and advice. He's totally a players' coach and a great leader."

Malloy asked Kwiatkowski about my promotion to assistant head coach at Montana State. "It was a way for us to keep him," Pete said. "Joe was getting offers from Portland State, and we anticipated that he would get more offers. Like I've said before, he was a rising star in the coaching ranks. Plus he was ready for the job."

The judge asked Pete if he, or anyone with the MSU football program, was aware of my involvement in the use and sale of meth. Pete said absolutely not. "[We] had no idea any of this was going on," he added, "none whatsoever."

Vicky talked about my relationship with her son and other MSU players when I was their coach. "He was a major influence on Adam and the others," she said. "He was a mentor to a lot of them. We consider Joe part of our family, that's how much we think of him."

I've known Haflich, the current head football coach at American River College in Sacramento, since he was my coach in high school. He told the court about some of the challenges I faced growing up in Pittsburg, saying I saw and experienced more adversity and disadvantages than anyone should. Despite the vices I indulged in and the transgressions I committed, Jerry said he and his wife, Rosanne, still believed in me as a person and a coach. "I don't know if you could find a better young coach than Joe O'Brien," he stated.

When the speakers finished Malloy turned to me. "Do you have anything to say before I sentence you?" he asked.

"Yes, your honor," I replied. I stood up and took a deep breath. I had a speech prepared, but after the third or fourth sentence I become emotional, my voice cracked, and I had to stop momentarily to gather myself. I started again, trying to blink back the tears as I spoke.

"Football has been my passion for 31 years. And I've lost that forever, and I did it to myself. I now understand how it can all be lost if wrong choices are made. I stand before you today a shameful man." I proceeded to apologize to everyone: Gracie, my players, my fellow coaches, and the fans and supporters of Montana State.

When I finished, Molloy thanked me for my comments and sincerity. The judge then asked Dan Buckley if he had anything to add. "No, your honor," my attorney replied. "I agree with you. I think my client's apology was heartfelt and well thought out."

"Anything from the prosecutor?" Malloy asked. Joshua Van de Wetering stood up. "Yes, your honor," he said. "I've heard it all before. And I take exception to O'Brien trying to distinguish himself as not just another criminal. We have to treat O'Brien like every other criminal that comes in here, because that's what he is. Sure, he apologized to a lot of people today. But what about the unknown number of drug users who consumed the estimated 360 grams of meth he brought into Gallatin County? He infested the Bozeman area with drugs. How many people were turned onto meth because of Mr. O'Brien? Where is his apology to them?"

The judge duly noted the U.S. attorney's comments and said he was prepared to make his ruling. I got up from my chair and faced the man who was about to decide my fate. My heart was pounding as I awaited his next few words.

Molloy dispensed with any more drama, sentencing me to four years in prison and eight years probation. "I listened to those who spoke about you today, and I read all of the 20 letters written on your behalf," he said. "I've read all the pre-sentence reports, and I've struggled with this decision.

"It almost seems like you're two different people. On one hand, I see a respected, up-and-coming coach who was quickly rising through the ranks at the college level. On the other hand, part of you was engaged with the underworld, the dirty underbelly of society. ... You are like Achilles, destroyed by your own choices."

Molloy went on, saying he recognized my professional accomplishments as well as my natural inclination and ability to coach. But those attributes and my celebrity, he stated, did not mitigate the seriousness of my crimes. "I've known about you from your days of playing at Boise State. I know exactly who you are and your role at Montana State. I know that you guys beat Montana [the previous two seasons], and I'm a big Grizzly fan. But I'm not going to hold that against you."

His words broke some of the tension as a few chuckles emanated from the back of the courtroom.

"Seriously, I remember you said in your speech that your life is over and your coaching career is over," the judge continued. "I'm a football fan, but there's more to life than football. You may not realize it now, but you've got a lot more to live for, and you've got a lot more going for you than just coaching."

My punishment included a $23,442 fine and 500 hours of community service. Molloy also said he was going to recommend me for the federal prison system's Residential Drug Abuse and boot camp programs, which is what I was hoping for. I knew I wouldn't be eligible for RDAP without a documented drug abuse problem, and when I tested positive for meth during my court appearance in May, the judge had sufficient grounds to make his recommendation.

"Not only will I recommend you for RDAP because I think you need it, but if boot camp is available at the institution that you're held, I'm going to recommend you for that program, too," he said. "In fact, not only will I recommend you, you'll probably end up running the damn thing."

His comment again elicited muffled laughter from the gallery.

Realizing I was probably headed for prison, I had sold my house several weeks earlier and had a chunk of the money with me. Buckley asked to speak: "Your honor, my client has a check for $18,000. He is prepared to forfeit the entire amount now as part of his fine."

"Excuse me?" said a surprised Malloy.

"That's correct, your honor," Buckley said. "May I approach the bench?"

I wanted to show the judge up front that I was serious about making reparations. I knew such fines are rarely paid entirely until a convict has done his time, and never, to my knowledge, at a sentencing. Buckley explained my intentions to the judge. "My client wants to pay as much of the fine as possible now. He doesn't want any outstanding bills upon his release." Molloy nodded and told my lawyer to step back. The judge addressed the court.

"Well, this has never happened before in my court," he said. "Usually if you give restitution while in prison, you pay something like $10 a month. I've changed my mind regarding the fine. Mr. O'Brien, assuming this check is good I will accept it as full payment of your fine and suspend the remaining balance of what you owe."

Immediately following my hearing Victor Rodriguez was sentenced to five years and 10 months in prison, Melissa Strain was sentenced to three years behind bars, and Matthew Monts got two years. Although we were tried as co-conspirators, we never saw each other during the proceedings, and all our hearings and our sentencings were carried out separately.

I LOOKED AT Gracie as I was led out of the courtroom in handcuffs. We were both in tears. I was worried and upset, but at the same time a feeling of immense relief washed over me. The waiting was over. I no longer had to wonder, worry and speculate. I knew what I had to do; now at least I knew what I was dealing with. It made everything easier to accept. And The Lie continued to fade.

Given his options I thought Molloy made a just and fair ruling. Going into the courtroom that day, I was praying for a sentence of five years or less. Based on Molloy's record and talking to other prisoners, I knew he was no bleeding heart; I met drug dealers whom he had sentenced to 10, 15, 20 and, in one case, 30 years in prison. But most of them were re-peat offenders while others committed their crimes using violence and/or weapons, neither of which applied in my case. One inmate told me that in many federal courts, the possession of a gun in a drug case adds an almost automatic 10 years to a convict's sentence. Judge Donald Molloy helped save me that day by giving me hope with a prison sentence that I could live with.

And Gracie gave me something even more important that day—a reason to live. I was prepared to do my time and get out of prison as soon as possible so I could be with her for the rest of my life. A few hours after my sentencing we talked on the phone. "We can do this," she said. "We can get through this together." That's all the incentive I needed to get through what was to be a long, lonely and difficult ordeal. I was determined to do it. "OK," I said to myself. "I know what I'm in for. I've got to make the best of it. I've got to take this sentence and cut into it in every way possible. I've got to do this for Gracie and me."

FROM MOLLOY'S COURTROOM I was taken to the Missoula County Jail. Including the five months I spent in the Jefferson County Jail before my sentencing I was moved a dozen times and held in eight detention centers in five states—county jails in Boulder, Helena, Great Falls (twice), and Shelby, Montana; federal holding facilities in Seattle and Oklahoma City (twice); and federal prisons in Las Vegas and Herlong, California—before I finally landed in the U.S. Penitentiary at Lewisburg in Pennsylvania the following summer.

The time I spent in the Montana jails was the worst. They were cramped, dingy and oppressive. In November 2004 I was flown from Se-attle to the federal transport station in Oklahoma City with a group of federal prisoners. A few weeks later I was sent to Nellis Prison Camp, a minimum-security facility near Las Vegas. Nellis was a major improve-ment and a welcomed change from the repressive jails in Montana. It had a gym and a weight room, outdoor facilities that included softball and football fields, and better food. I even got to coach a prison basketball team while I was there. Because the Federal Bureau of Prisons does its best to place inmates in facilities as close as possible to their home, I initially thought Las Vegas might be my final destination. But around the same time as my arrival, the government announced that it planned to shut down Nellis, which it did in 2006.

The federal prison system started reassigning prisoners from Las Vegas, and in the spring of 2005, thanks in part to my experience with the roofing company in Bozeman, I was among approximately 150 low-risk, non-violent inmates who were transferred from Nellis to the new medium-security federal correctional institution in Herlong, much of which was still under construction. I was assigned to do electrical, HVAC and roofing work; I also was part of the work crew that built the prison's football and softball fields and erected the barbwire fences. Gracie visited me twice in Las Vegas and once in Herlong, and Jerry and Rosanne Haflich also came to see me in Herlong. The northern California facility, however, wasn't my final stop, and for the second time I was transported to Oklahoma City.

THROUGHOUT MY INCARCERATION I did everything I could to stay out of trouble and maintain a clean record. I was focused on doing my time and getting out. My second stay in Oklahoma City, however, was very frustrating. The jail there is a holding facility and not designed for lengthy stays. For some reason, my time there grew from days to weeks. There was limited outdoor access, the ventilation was bad, and I was feeling especially pent-up and angry.

And one day I snapped.

As a convict in the federal prison system, I had to regularly share my cell with another inmate, and throughout my confinement I'd deliver the same message with each new cellmate: "I don't want to tell you about my case, and I don't want hear about yours. Just be respectful of me, and I'll be respectful to you, and we'll have no problem."

I was sitting in my cell one day when the correctional officers brought in a new guy to share my space. I could tell he was bad news from the start.

He mouthed off and cussed at the COs as they pushed him into the cell. He was a real lowlife, a scruffy, skinny redneck with long hair, a big mouth, and a real attitude. He told me he was a truck driver and got busted for drug possession. I politely gave my standard admonition, but he started telling me his story anyway. "Listen," I said. "Didn't you hear what I said? I'm not interested in your case."

"Fuck you," he replied as he climbed up on the top bunk bed. "It's a free country. I'll talk if I want to." He proceeded to tell me that while he was on the road in Louisiana he picked up a young woman—an escapee from a mental-health institution. He said he had some meth and other drugs. I told him to shut up, but he continued, bragging that he plied his passenger with some of his drugs, beat and raped her, and threw her off his rig at a truck stop in Texas.

"What did you just say?" I said.

"You heard me," he replied. "What the fuck are you going to do about it?"

"So you're proud of what you did?" I said. "You know what? You're a piece of shit."

"Fuck you!" he snapped. "What the hell do you care about some fuckin' retard?!"

I just lost it. I jumped from my chair, grabbed him by his hair, and punched him in the face. Then I grabbed the back of his head and proceeded to slam his face against the steel bracket of the upper bunk. Blood gushed all over the cell. I knew I was in deep shit. I had about an hour to clean the guy up as best I could before we were released from our cells for dinner.

When the cell doors opened, I grabbed the redneck by his collar. "You better tell the guards that you fell and fucked up your face," I hissed, "and you're not coming back to this cell, because if you do I'm going to fuckin' kill you."

The guy's face was a mess. It was obvious that his injuries were not the result of a fall. While we were eating dinner, the redneck went to a CO. I could see him talking to the guard and pointing at me. Normally prisoners don't stay in places like Oklahoma City long enough to become acquainted with other inmates or the COs, but because of my extended stay, I got to know a few of the guards as well as a couple of fellow prisoners, one of whom was sitting next to me.

"Oh shit," I said to my dinner companion. "They're going to send me to the fuckin' 'hole'"—the term for solitary confinement, where inmates who have committed acts of violence and other serious offenses are kept away from the rest of the prison population in eight-by-10-foot windowless cells with just a narrow bunk and a metal toilet.

"Do me a favor," I said. "Here's Gracie's phone number. First chance you get, please call her and tell her she won't be hearing from me for a while. I beat the shit out of the guy in my cell. I guarantee he's telling the guards. Don't tell Gracie what happened; just tell her I'll call her when I can."

After dinner the redneck and I returned to our cell; a few minutes later six correctional officers appeared. Without a word they unlocked the door and barged in; I was positive they were going to grab me and haul me away. Instead, they grabbed the redneck, shackled him, and took him away. About a minute later, there was an announcement over the loudspeaker. It was the shift supervisor, one of the corrections officers I knew: "O'Brien," he bellowed, "I want you in my office, right now!" I was escorted to the guard station at the end of the cellblock.

When I got to the supervisor's office he slammed the door closed. It was just the two of us. "Goddamn it, O'Brien," he said, "if I didn't know you, your ass would be in the fuckin' hole! If you want to get out of prison as soon as you can this sure as hell isn't the way you do it! You don't go beating the shit out of your cellmate! All you had to do is come to me and say you didn't want to share a cell with that asshole!"

"Yeah, I fucked up," I responded. "No excuse other than I'm stressed and pissed off, and then that guy starts telling me about—"

The supervisor interrupted me. "Yeah, I know," he said, holding a file folder in his hand. "I don't usually read all the files of prisoners when they come in. It's not my job to pass judgment. But after what happened today, I pulled the guy's file."

He didn't tell me what was in the folder, but it was clear he knew about the redneck's alleged incident with the woman from Louisiana, as well as the rest of his criminal record. "Listen, I can see why you did what you did," he said in a soft voice. "I know why he's in here."

Then he paused. "I've got three daughters …" His voice tailed off. He looked at me. "Get the fuck out of here," he said. "Go back to your cell. If you pull anything like that again, I swear I'll send you to the hole."

CHAPTER
11

THE 2005 COLLEGE FOOTBALL SEASON would have been my eighth as a coach. It would have been my third year as Montana State's assistant head coach. Or maybe by then I would have moved up the coaching ladder, as many people predicted, to a defensive coordinator's position at another school. Or maybe—just maybe—after the '05 season I would have returned to Boise State with MSU D-coordinator Pete Kwiatkowski to join new head coach Chris Petersen.

Instead, I was Federal Bureau of Prisons inmate No. 07167-046 at the United States Penitentiary at Lewisburg, a high-security correctional institution in central Pennsylvania, the final stop of my 28-month imprisonment.

Captivity is crushing, degrading and frightening. It can be fraught with dread that is almost suffocating. It can drain you to the point where you fight to keep your sanity. For some guys it was a losing battle. Confinement can make you lose the will to live; I saw it every day in dozens of faces—from ruthless, violent felons to harmless computer geeks who were doing time for white-collar crimes.

When I arrived at USP Lewisburg in the summer of 2005 I decided I wasn't going to let it get the best of me. Soon after my incarceration by the federal government 15 months earlier in Butte, Montana, I figured there were two ways to approach my prison term: I could seethe, blame others for my misfortune, do as little as possible, and make life difficult for those around me. Or I could use my time behind bars to cleanse myself—mentally, physically and spiritually—and make myself a better person.

I chose the latter.

But it didn't happen overnight. Fortunately, Lewisburg had four things that helped me cope: the federal prison system's Residential Drug Abuse program, a modicum of freedom, a daily routine, and regular recreational outlets.

BECAUSE RDAP IS designed to reward successful participants with reductions to their sentences, entry into the program is in high demand—even among inmates without substance-abuse problems. Ironically, with one exception—in May 2004, a few days before my court hearing in Butte—I entered the program having not used drugs in almost two years. Yet the reason I got into RDAP was because of that one time I *did* use methamphetamine. If the urine test I took that day in the courthouse hadn't detected traces of meth in my system, federal judge Donald Molloy would have had no compelling reason to recommend me for RDAP at my sentencing five months later. But he did, and my participation in the program eventually shaved nine months off my sentence.

I also had hoped to get into Lewisburg's boot camp to trim my sentence even further, but the Federal Bureau of Prisons eliminated its "intensive confinement" program a few months earlier. Consequently, beyond earning reduced time for good behavior RDAP became the only means by which I could receive a reduction in my sentence.

I pondered my options, fell back on my coaching experience, and devised a game plan. Designed to hasten my release, my plan was based on four R's: recovery, rehabilitation, renewal and redemption.

As a low-risk, non-violent, first-time offender I was assigned to Lewisburg's satellite minimum-security "camp," which is a separate facility from the main, maximum-security complex. Compared to the other jails, prisons and detention centers where I was held, Lewisburg's 700-bed camp seemed like a luxury hotel. At the other places, I was kept in a cell and locked up like a caged animal as I moved from jail to jail. The camp was considerably more accommodating. Instead of cells, the camp's living quarters were like military barracks. The absence of bars and the open space made all the difference in the world. We were allowed minor conveniences that I used to take for granted. If you had to take a leak in the middle of the night, all you had to do was get up, walk down the hall to the restroom, relieve yourself, and return to bed. In the morning you could get up early, leave the barracks, run or walk laps at the nearby track, return to the building, take a shower, have some breakfast, and be ready for work.

As long as we were at certain places at certain times—at 4 p.m., for example, there was a daily prisoner count—we had free access to most of the compound. It wasn't a large area and there weren't a lot of places to roam, but the mere freedom to move about relatively unsupervised was invigorating and gratifying.

In stark contrast to the main penitentiary with its soaring walls, razor wire and looming watchtowers, the camp seemed "more like converted elementary school grounds," wrote Andrew Hinkelman of the *Bozeman Daily Chronicle*, who did a story about my time in Lewisburg. Unlike the main pen, which held about 1,400 inmates at the time, the camp's "entire vibe is different, more relaxed," Hinkelman wrote. "No walls or razor wire or even a locked door. It looked as if an inmate were so inclined, he could walk out the front door."

Sure, the captivity was tough and sometimes depressing, but I believe God doesn't put you in any position that you can't handle. Because of the adversity I have experienced throughout my life, I think I'm mentally and physically equipped to withstand hardship and misfortune. I wasn't going to let my imprisonment break my spirit, and I was big and physically strong enough that I wasn't too worried about any problems or confrontations that might arise. Because of my strong personality, I quickly gained a fair amount of respect throughout the camp, even among those who didn't particularly like me.

I only resorted to violence once during my stay in Lewisburg. The inmates in RDAP bunk together, and one member of our group was a guy around 20 years old and a bit of a punk with a smart mouth. He was constantly annoying a lot of us with his singing and rapping. One day he was being particularly irritating. "Hey, asshole, don't come by my bunk making that noise," I said. "I'm sick of it." But he ignored my request and blithely continued with his rapping. A few days later a group of us were gathered near the complex softball diamond. I called the rapper over and said I wanted to talk to him about something in the dugout. As soon as we were out of the correctional officers' sight, I punched him in the face twice and threw him to the ground. "Listen, I'm not kidding," I growled. "Knock that shit off, or next time you'll *really* get a beating." He didn't sing or rap around me again. Like the shift supervisor in Oklahoma City, the rapper could have derailed my hope for an early release had he reported my violent outburst, but fortunately he didn't.

Getting into a routine was vital to my physical and mental health. Without a set schedule, days in prison can seem to drag on forever. The more I kept busy, the better my frame of mind. I was determined to keep myself occupied—perform my duties, attend my RDAP meetings, pursue my pastimes—and not sit still for a single moment until my head hit the pillow each night at 10:30. I saw guys who just languished in prison. I saw their hair fall out in patches; I saw them age 10 years in six months. I was not going to let that happen to me.

I started out working two jobs—as a cook and a janitor. As a cook I would get up at 4:30 in the morning to prepare breakfast and lunch for about 260 inmates. My specialty was soups, mostly chicken and beef. It was a good gig because I could get extra food. My janitorial duties included mopping, buffing and waxing the floors in an area of the minimum-security unit for about 17 cents an hour.

Thanks to my skills as an electrician, I eventually landed a job with the prison's electrical and HVAC work unit, and in my final months at Lewisburg I proposed and spearheaded a roofing project that would provide the primary motivation for me to start my own general contracting/roofing/siding business in Great Falls, Montana, after my release. Lewisburg has a program that repairs and refurbishes abandoned and stolen bicycles, which were housed and fixed in an old and dilapidated warehouse. The penitentiary itself was more than 70 years old, and this particular structure looked like one of the original buildings. I was in the building one day in the spring of 2006 when I noticed that the roof was in serious need of repair; when it rained there were leaks everywhere.

Knowing I had the expertise to put a new roof on the building, I submitted a work request to the warden, asking if I could take on the project. Some of my fellow inmates thought I was crazy. "Joe, you're probably outta here in a few months," one of them said. "Just put in your time and get the hell out of here. Why bother?" But I knew the busier I stayed, the better I coped. When my request was approved I assembled a work crew and we reroofed the building in no time. It looked like it had been done by a professional outfit, if I do say so myself.

My routine changed slightly because of my jobs, but a typical day started with work in the morning followed by RDAP counseling sessions in the early afternoon. Late afternoon and early evening hours were for weightlifting and other recreation. At night I maintained my routine: I'd play spades for about an hour with a couple of fellow inmates, watch some TV, and hit the sack.

As a former coach, I became highly involved in Lewisburg's sports and recreation programs. I taught strength training and coached softball and flag football teams (although "flag" football in prison is a misnomer; it is as dirty and violent as it gets). "To take control of a group of inmates is one of the toughest things I've ever done, but it's been a great experience," I told the *Bozeman Daily Chronicle*'s Hinkelman. At the beginning, some of the cons were taken aback by my excitable, blunt coaching style. "But these guys will soak up any knowledge you can give them," I said. "Any advantage these guys can get on anybody, they're going to listen." I knew what made them tick and how to motivate them, and I believe several of them benefited from my guidance.

I BEGAN TO write, and I read more. I tried to make myself more informed and more thoughtful; I prayed and tried to make myself better. I started a journal, wrote about football coaching techniques, jotted down memories of my childhood, all sorts of things. I started reading the Bible, among other books. I spent time in honest self-reflection, and I prayed some more.

When I was growing up, my parents weren't big on God or religion. But as a nine-year-old living in Custer, South Dakota, I had my first exposure to Christianity. One of my friends was the son of the pastor of a small church, and I regularly attended Sunday services with them during the one year I lived there. I always believed in God, but He didn't become an important part of my life until I ended up in prison. Like many people who have been to the edge of the abyss, I sought divine intervention as a last resort. And like many convicts, prison was where I rediscovered my faith. I didn't go overboard, but I started attending some of the prison's Bible studies and church services. And as the weeks and months passed I read the Bible more and began to pray on a daily basis. And The Lie—with all its falsehoods, instant gratification and selfishness—continued to fade.

I had hours upon hours by myself, so I prayed a lot—for another opportunity ... for Gracie, that she would remain strong ... for the perseverance to use my time in prison as a learning opportunity and to not lash out in anger and frustration ... to stay the course throughout RDAP's intensive therapy ... for the resolve to remain drug-free ... for the day I would be free again ... for the opportunity to repair the damage I had done ... to someday coach again.

"I pray daily on that," I told Hinkelman. "That someone will give me the opportunity to do what I love the most. I made mistakes that were costly and embarrassing and terrible. But I'm a good coach. It's my passion; it's what I love to do. It's something that I do daily, even here. It's something in my blood that I enjoy; something I was getting to be really good at."

I also alluded to an interest in someday telling my story in a book or as a public speaker. "[O'Brien] knows getting back on the football field will take time, if it happens at all," Hinkelman wrote. "But he does have a plan to at least interact again with student-athletes. O'Brien wants to become a motivational speaker, delivering his personal story to administrators and players alike. [He] hopes to reach the kid—or coach—who feels like he or she can't address the problems in front of them."

I've heard just about every tale of woe imaginable from the cons I lived with, I told Hinkelman—and all those stories had nothing on mine. "To this day, I've never heard a message even near the one that I am going to give," I said. "I've seen a lot of things and I've done a lot of things, good and bad; I just think it's a unique message that needs to get out there."

During my time in Lewisburg I tried to re-establish my relationship with my eight-year-old daughter, Haley, by giving her an occasional phone call. But I always had to cut our conversations short because I didn't want her to know I was in prison. After seven minutes an inmate's telephone conversation is interrupted with the recording, "This is a call from the Lewisburg Penitentiary." Each time I called Haley, who lives with her mother in Virginia, I had to time my conversation on my watch and end it before that dreaded intrusion. I don't know whether or not my ex-wife told our daughter where I was calling from, but I still took it upon myself to make sure Haley didn't find out from me.

"I've wasted a lot of time in my daughter's life," I told Hinkelman. "I wasn't involved as much in her life before I came to prison because of ego-driven issues. And obviously putting myself in a situation like this wasted another couple years."

"It's that kind of blunt honesty as a motivational speaker [O'Brien] hopes can change some lives for the better," Hinkelman wrote. "And he hopes that sort of contrition will get him a second chance to coach again."

I also phoned Gracie on a regular basis. Inmates are allowed 300 minutes of telephone time a month, an average of 10 minutes a day. Gracie and I learned to talk quickly and tried to settle any differences we might have within those precious 10 or so minutes because it would kill me if we ended our conversation on a quarrelsome or unpleasant note. A couple of times I used up my 300 minutes with more than a week still remaining in the month. Being cut off from Gracie for eight or nine days was agonizing. It made the hours and days crawl. Gracie remained my main incentive for an early release. The thought of having her back in my arms continued to get me through the difficult and lonely times.

Throughout my stay in Lewisburg I worked diligently to meet my RDAP requirements and remained on my best behavior, the dustup with the rapper notwithstanding. In early 2006 the Federal Bureau of Prisons set my tentative release date for sometime in September of that year, roughly 20 months ahead of schedule.

In May of that year I hit the minimum-security inmate's jackpot: a 36-hour furlough—my first taste of freedom in two years. Gracie flew from Montana to Pennsylvania, rented a car, and picked me up on a Friday morning. We got a motel room, shopped at a mall, and went to a nice restaurant. "Hang in there, Joe," she said over dinner that night. "We're almost done with this thing. Just another four months." Then she added, "You better not get in trouble and do more time in there." I decided not to tell her about my little incident with the rapper in the softball dugout.

It was painful and emotional when we said goodbye outside Lewisburg's gates on Saturday night, but my time with Gracie just made me more determined to get through my sentence as soon as possible. I can't put into words how wonderful it was to be with her. It's a cliché, but you find out who loves you and who doesn't when you're at your lowest points in life. That's one reason why I love Gracie so much.

ON WEDNESDAY SEPT. 20, 2006, I was released from USP Lewisburg. I was excited but calm as I walked through the penitentiary gates, boarded a bus, and headed to Pittsburgh (Pennsylvania, not California), where I would meet Gracie and continue our trip via Greyhound to Great Falls. The pittance I made during my 13 months in the pen barely covered basic purchases in the commissary, so when I was released my only possessions were the $10 in my pocket and the clothes I was wearing, which Gracie sent me. I didn't look back as the bus departed.

I got off in a small town about 45 miles from the prison to switch buses. It felt strange to be standing outside a small bus station by myself—unchained, unsupervised, unimpeded—in the middle of rural Pennsylvania. I walked across the street from the station to a convenience store and bought some grape-flavored hard candy; it was the sweetest morsel I had ever tasted in my life. I breathed deeply and smelled real freedom for the first time in two years and four months. The feeling was sublime.

I boarded another bus for the five-hour trip to the depot in downtown Pittsburgh, where Gracie, who had taken a train from Montana, was waiting. My mind raced as the bus moved across the rolling hills of Pennsylvania: "Is this really happening?" I asked myself. "Will things work out between Gracie and me? What will I do for a living? Will I be a different person?"

The Federal Bureau of Prisons gave me the option to fly or bus to Great Falls, where I would be required to spend six months in a residential re-entry center, also known as a halfway house, as part of my RDAP early-release agreement. Gracie and I chose the latter because we were in no hurry. Throughout our 1,800-mile journey I had to keep pinching myself, finding it hard to believe I was finally free and sitting with this beautiful young woman who had stayed with me through my darkest days.

When we reached Great Falls three days later I was met at the bus depot by a counselor with the Great Falls Transition Center—the halfway house where I was scheduled to reside for the next six months as part of my mandatory outpatient drug and alcohol rehab treatment. During my stay at the center I worked for Gracie's dad, Tom Duffy, a Great Falls businessman. During the day I worked in Tom's furniture store and on a house he was building for $8 an hour, returning to the halfway house each night.

I had another reduction to my sentence after four months when my status was upgraded to "home confinement," which allowed me to move out of the halfway house for the final eight weeks of my program. As I prepared for my transfer from the prison system to the federal probation program, Gracie and I stayed in a trailer on the property where I was helping to build her dad's house. It was a pretty convenient arrangement. I would wake up, have some breakfast, and walk about 30 yards to work. During the final phase of my detention program I was free to go anywhere I pleased as long as I was back in the trailer each day by 9 p.m.

WHEN GRACIE AND I discussed where we would live following my release from prison, her hometown of Great Falls was a logical choice. For Gracie, it provided a solid support system that included her parents and many other friends and relatives. For me, it was the transition center and its rehab program, which met the requirements for my early-release agreement. One drawback was Great Falls' relative proximity (190 miles) to Bozeman, where I remained a pariah among many of the Montana State faithful.

Given my relative celebrity and the notoriety of my transgressions, Gracie and I knew there would be the occasional but inevitable glares and looks of disapproval and disdain when I was out in public—even in and around Great Falls. However, we both agreed that living somewhere else would just be running away from our problems. "When O'Brien walks around in public in Montana, people stare," wrote the *Idaho Statesman*'s Mike Prater in 2009. "He loathes the grocery store. Some appreciate what he did for Montana State football. Many more despise him for tarnishing the program's name."

In March 2007 I completed my early-release agreement and began my eight-year probation. With the exception of my one slipup in May 2004, I had not used illicit drugs in nearly four years. I was healthy, happy, grounded and well on my way to successful recovery and rehabilitation from substance abuse. That's not to say, however, that I've won the battle. There is never an end in recovery. It requires daily vigilance.

The following month I took an important step on my road to renewal and redemption when I spoke publicly for the first time about "Dealing with the Demons" at Carroll College.

Despite my comments in the *Bozeman Daily Chronicle* 10 months earlier about wanting to share my story, I was a bit apprehensive when Carroll College athletic director Bruce Parker first approached me about speaking to a gathering of college and high school student-athletes and coaches at the Helena, Montana, school. To help others avoid similar misfortune, part of me wanted to tell anyone who would listen about my missteps and mistakes. Yet another part wanted to bury the past, not relive it. I mean, who wants to dredge up a lifetime of bad decisions: 15 years of drug abuse, a period of distributing meth, a derailed coaching career, and 28 months in federal prison? However, realizing the good such a presentation might do, I agreed to Parker's proposal.

Through my years as a college and pro athlete and a coach, I became pretty good at speaking to large groups. But this talk would be completely different. Instead of getting up to deliver one of those canned, feel-good messages about team unity and athletic glory, which I could practically do in my sleep, I had been asked to talk about my dark side. I was accustomed to charming boosters and providing the media with helpful sound bites; now I was asked to bare my soul and tell hundreds of strangers—most of them impressionable young men and women—about my mistakes.

Like many speakers, I have my tried-and-true bromides, but when I talk to groups I usually do so without a whole lot of preparation. I find I do a better job if I speak from the heart. I was not completely sure what I was going to say as I made the 90-mile trip from Great Falls to Helena, nor did I know what the crowd's reaction would be. But I realized that the large audience certainly had to include at least a few young adults who were dealing with their own demons. "If I open up to these kids and share my experiences and discuss my poor choices, maybe I'll prod someone who needs help to get help," I thought as I drove along Interstate 15. "Maybe what I say tonight will make a difference to somebody."

That evening, I felt an inner peace as I walked to the podium and stood in front of the audience; it seemed like fate had brought me to that specific time and place. I'm not particularly eloquent, but the words just flowed. I touched upon my dysfunctional upbringing … my father's heroin overdose … my drug abuse at an early age … how I used meth and GHB … my hidden life … how I finally got caught … my time in prison.

I told the more than 400 student-athletes and coaches that the best way to avoid similar mistakes was to seek help right away. It wasn't a particularly original piece of advice, but it seemed to resonate with some of them. "It's a cliché, but you first have to admit to yourself that you have a problem and then do something about it," I said. "In prison they have a saying: You don't change because you see the light, you change because you feel the heat. I'm here to talk to you so you don't have to feel that heat.

If you have a problem like I did, don't do what I did, which was nothing. I didn't seek help. I should have. You have people who care about you: parents, coaches, friends, teammates, teachers. If you are dealing with a problem, talk to someone ... anyone. That's the first step. That's the step I didn't take until it was too late."

Parker later called my talk "very inspiring." On the website of the marketing firm that sponsors my motivational speeches, the Carroll AD wrote that my "hard-hitting" presentation would have "an everlasting effect on all of us. [Joe] was and is an outstanding football coach and motivator. He made a number of poor decisions in his life and has paid the price. He has truly learned his life's lessons and does a tremendous job telling his story. [His speech was] very thought-provoking and will definitely have an effect on the audiences' decision-making as well as their thought process."

The speech had a truly cathartic effect on me, and Parker's comments reinforced my belief that I had a story to tell and a message to share.

I CONTINUED TO work for Tom Duffy in Great Falls that spring. One day he gave me some sound business advice. "You know, you're really good at roofing," he said. "I'm guessing it's not something you want to do for the rest of your life, but why don't you try it and see where it gets you as far as making a living? If things don't work out, you can still work for me. I'll keep you on the payroll." It was a wonderful gesture by Gracie's dad. I had peace of mind knowing that I would have work, no matter what.

Gracie was working in the ad department of the *Great Falls Tribune* and our expenses were low. So I decided to take the plunge and start my roofing business in June 2007. I used my initials as part of its name: Get The J.O'B Done. Around the same time I took another kind of plunge: I proposed to Gracie. But first I shared my intentions with Tom and his wife, Cindy, who gave me their blessing to marry their daughter.

Like many startup businesses Get The J.O'B Done began on a shoestring budget and got off to a slow start. Then Mother Nature did me a big favor that summer. I was in the middle of my second roofing job when a vicious hailstorm ripped through Great Falls and did millions of dollars of damage to buildings throughout the area, especially to roofs. In the wake of the storm I had steady work for the next six months and repaired or replaced about two dozen roofs.

Get The J.O'B Done quickly earned a reputation for doing quality work at a competitive price, and in 2008, despite the nation's economic struggles, I expanded my services to general contracting and siding and employed as many as 10 workers at one time. Moreover, I extended my service area, accepting jobs as far away as Bozeman. Get The J.O'B Done was awarded major contracts such as a $675,000 project to refurbish the interior and exterior of a county building. In my business' first three years, my crews and I repaired or replaced more than 300 roofs in western Montana.

Gracie and I bought a 94-year-old house near downtown Great Falls and spent a year renovating our new home and planning our wedding. On June 7, 2008, we tied the knot in the Great Falls First United Methodist Church, where Gracie and her family worshiped when she was growing up. Among the 350 guests were my grandmother and Uncle Gary. Jon Montoya, a star defensive end who played for me at Montana State and is now a youth minister with Grace Bible Church in Bozeman, officiated the ceremony.

Along with Jon, the men in our wedding party would have made a pretty good football team. Ted Rivera, a former teammate of mine at Santa Clara, was my best man while the groomsmen included three of my former coaching colleagues at Montana State—Pete Kwiatkowski, Rob Christoff and Brock Berryhill—along with Jerry Haflich, a Sacramento State Hall of Fame linebacker. Jerry's daughter (and my goddaughter), Whitney, was also in our wedding party.

Our wedding day was glorious. I wanted all the attention to be on Gracie, and boy was it ever! By the time we got married I had known Gracie for six years, and I had never seen her more beautiful than that day. She was glowing. I never felt such joy, and it was because I knew she was happy.

Life was great. I was happily married to the best person I ever met, The Lie was becoming a distant memory, and my business was paying the bills and keeping me busy. But there was something still missing.

CHAPTER
12

GET THE J.O'B DONE HAS BEEN A BLESSING. It has been personally fulfilling and financially rewarding to own and operate a solvent and respected business. It also provides Gracie and me with a steady source of income and has filled me with a blue-collar sense of pride and accomplishment. I derive great satisfaction from working hard, repairing broken buildings, getting my hands dirty, and making an honest living. But God didn't put me here to repair roofs or install siding.

Coaching is my calling.

"Calling," as defined by *Webster's*, is a "strong inner impulse toward a particular course of action especially when accompanied by conviction and divine influence." Those words certainly capture the essence of what I believe to be my calling—and what I hope leads me to a successful return to the coaching profession. It took me nearly half a lifetime, but I now have gained balance in my life and have attained the proper perspective to move forward thanks to the "divine influence" that guides me along the right path. My initial "course of action" was obscured by years of substance abuse and hampered by bad decisions, but my calling now answers to—and is guided by—a higher power.

I'm determined, but I'm not foolish: I know I'm a parolee seeking work in a profession that usually requires a squeaky-clean resume. I know there are people—especially within the Montana State community—who will react angrily to my intentions; I've heard the hue and cry: *He coached young men while he used and sold drugs! He's a convicted felon! He can't be trusted! He made a mockery of the profession he supposedly loves!*

I don't take such criticism and resentment lightly. I know methamphetamine is a scourge upon our society. I acknowledge that I did serious damage to the MSU athletic program that exacted a toll on many people. I apologize for those mistakes; I'm sorry that I hurt people who believed in and trusted me. I wish I could, but I can't go back and undo any of those mistakes. And I will state here one more time: Yes, I was part of a drug ring that brought meth into Bozeman, but I never offered, exposed or even mentioned meth to anyone having anything to do with the university or MSU athletics. If some people want to maintain a grudge and can't find it within their hearts to forgive me, all I can say is this: I went to prison for what I did. I paid my dues, did my time, and learned my lesson.

I know that men who go to prison for using and selling meth don't usually end up coaching college or pro football. Even though I've kicked my habit, cleaned up my act, and paid my proverbial debt to society, the stigma of past wrongdoing remains, and some people still think I don't deserve a second chance. I know the odds are against me, but I'm determined to start anew and do everything possible to reach my goal to be the coach God meant me to be. And thanks to my friend, fellow coach, and former Boise State teammate Brian Smith, I have already started my comeback bid with two coaching stints in arena football—first in Fresno, California, in 2009 and then in Wenatchee, Washington, in 2011.

BEFORE I JOINED Smith in Fresno as a volunteer coach with the Central Valley Coyotes of Arena Football League 2, I first looked into coaching at the high school level in western Montana. With my fledgling business to run, I wanted to remain in the Great Falls area while at the same time testing the waters for a possible return to coaching in some capacity.

Turns out the water wasn't even tepid. I knew my chances were slim to none, but I didn't expect such an icy response. I inquired about or applied for at least eight coaching positions in 2007 and '08; in most cases I wasn't even given a return call. Even Jack Johnson, the estimable head football coach at Great Falls' C.M. Russell High School, couldn't help me. Johnson, who has won 77 percent of his games at CMR since he took over as the school's head coach in 1972, expressed an interest in having me join his staff, but school officials told him not to bother. Similarly, my friend Jerry Haflich, the head football coach at American River College, wanted to hire me as an assistant, but his hands were tied by a state law that prohibits anyone with a drug-distribution conviction from coaching at the high school or junior college level. Jerry submitted an appeal, but administrators at the two-year school turned down his request.

I don't really blame those who have been unwilling or reluctant to hire me as a coach. I'm the first to acknowledge that it would take a certain amount of courage for a head coach, athletic director or other administrator to do so. Moreover, I know if I have any chance to return to coaching, it almost certainly will be at the college level or beyond. Nevertheless, I thought I might get a chance in 2008 when Gracie's brother, Conrad Duffy, was hired as head football coach at the high school in Cascade, Montana, a small farming and ranching town about 25 miles from Great Falls.

Conrad wanted to hire me, but his efforts were futile. School officials, however, said they would allow me to work with the team as a volunteer that fall under certain conditions: I could help with practices, but could only function on the periphery at the Badgers' games. Banned from the sidelines and locker room, I was relegated to the press box but not allowed to wear headphones. Given all those restrictions, I ostensibly served as team "videographer" and filmed the Badgers' games that season. During my brief involvement with the Cascade football team, I also started a booster organization that raised $3,000 toward the purchase of a big-screen TV, other video equipment, and new football jerseys and T-shirts.

At the end of the season I was asked to speak at the team's annual awards banquet. Unlike my presentation at Carroll College some 20 months earlier, my talk was not so much about dealing with the demons but more about lessons learned on the football field.

Sure, you had a rough season in terms of wins and losses, I told the players that night, but the unity you developed and the commitment you demonstrated as a team will translate into individual achievements later in life. I briefly mentioned my missteps, but my overall message to the players and the rest of the audience focused on the positive aspects of teamwork, dedication and a collective goal to improve. When I was finished, I received a standing ovation from the players. At the end of the evening, the team presented me with a football signed by all the players. Most of them hugged me, thanked me for my contribution to the program, and said how much they appreciated my speech.

After the season Conrad again broached the subject of hiring me, but his request was again denied. It was then I decided not to beat my head against a wall and focused my search on positions at the college or pro level.

IF I HAD just one word to assess my life so far, "almost" sums it up quite well: The internal turmoil born from a disjointed and dysfunctional upbringing *almost* sent me on a path to ruin. The methamphetamine, GHB and other drugs I abused for 15 years *almost* destroyed my life. I *almost* damaged numerous friendships and relationships beyond repair. The Lie *almost* did me in.

I *almost* lost everything.

Given the depths to which I sank and the public disgrace I endured, I think God *almost* didn't give me a second chance. But He has. Whether or not I reach my ultimate goal to coach college or pro football, I know my comeback attempt is a journey of atonement, and I hope my reclamation will serve as an example to others. Because of my past transgressions, I know my attempt to return to the profession I love will be a continuous process on two fronts: proving my worth as a coach and demonstrating my sobriety as a former drug addict.

Throughout 2008 I continued to build my business as I met prospective customers, submitted bids, consummated deals, and supervised projects. I put my head down and worked as hard as I could. At the time I just wanted to keep Get The J.O'B Done going, do quality work for my customers, make a decent living, and give Gracie the kind of life she deserved. But in the back of my mind the void in my life remained.

In early '09 Brian Smith, the defensive coordinator for af2's Central Valley Coyotes, asked if I might be interested in helping his team on a volunteer basis. Brian and I had not spoken in some time, but we immediately picked up where we left off.

"Joe and I kind of went our separate ways after I finished playing at Boise State in 1995," said Smith, who played for Edmonton in the Canadian Football League in 1996 and '97, a pro league in Germany in 1998, and four years of pro arena football. "After that, we were both pursuing coaching careers and lost contact for a while. But I was following his success at Montana State. In fact, when I was a player/coach in arena football in Boise and Kearney, Nebraska, and Joe was at MSU I was hoping to get a chance to coach there. With Joe, Pete [Kwiatkowski], Marcel Yates [another former Bronco on the MSU staff who is now Boise State's defensive backs coach], and Jay Dumas, a high school teammate of mine, I knew it was a really good group of guys. That staff reminded me of Pokey Allen's staff when Joe and I played at Boise State—guys like [assistants] Kwiatkowski, Ron Gould and Tom Mason. It would have been a perfect situation for me—then Joe had his problems with the law."

The timing of Smith's offer certainly helped. Roofing and construction work is pretty stagnant in Montana from November through springtime, and the 2009 af2 season was to begin in February. I received permission from my parole officer to relocate for a few months in Fresno and work as an unpaid consultant to Smith and head coach Fred Biletnikoff Jr.

In 2009 interviews with the *Contra Costa Times* and *Idaho Statesman*, Smith said he knew I was anxious to coach again and tried to convince Biletnikoff that they could use my help on the defensive side of the ball.

"It was a no-brainer," Brian told Jennifer Starks of the *Times*. "Joe is the hardest-working coach I've ever met." Around the same time he told the *Statesman*'s Mike Prater that it was time to move on and let me do what I was meant to do: "[Joe] is the first to admit that he's made mistakes, but he's willing to take it head-on," Smith said. "He's a great technician as a coach and he shows by example what hard work can do for you. It oozes out of every pore of his body."

Biletnikoff, son of the Hall of Fame wide receiver, echoed Smith's sentiments, saying my past mistakes were "100 percent irrelevant" once he realized I was genuinely committed to helping his team and could coach my ass off. "Everyone has a past," he told Starks. "This is professional football. There's no athletic director here, no parent club, none of those things that can weigh heavily on the circumstances of our pasts. This is professional football; we're dealing with grown men here."

As a teenager growing up in the mean streets of Tacoma, Washington, Smith had his own brushes with the law before he eventually became a team leader at Boise State, a two-time all-conference player for the Broncos, and an arena football head coach. The mistake-strewn paths Brian and I followed and the hard lessons we learned allowed us to impart more than X's and O's to the 2009 Central Valley players.

"This [af2] is a second-chance league," Smith said. "Players at this level have made mistakes—some on the field, some off. Many of them are looking for one more opportunity to play pro football; they certainly aren't in it for the money because they get no more than $250 a game. Unlike a lot of coaches, Joe and I can relate to our players because of what we both went through as young men.

"Some people will continue to bring up Joe's past. So be it. Of course there are consequences for your actions; Joe has addressed those consequences and is ready to move on. He fits in here because he is the kind of coach who not only will teach you about football, but also about life. He fell off the straight and narrow, and that makes him highly qualified to talk to our guys. What we can teach these players is bigger than football—much bigger than Brian Smith and Joe O'Brien. What we are doing is giving lots of guys a second chance at life in a second-chance league.

"It was, and is, Joe's work ethic and his commitment to excellence and believing in yourself that made him such a good teammate and what makes him an outstanding coach," Smith continued. "I think back to 1994 at Boise State and watching him train, work out, and play every down like it was his last. He was on top of his game every day. I am certain that what we learned and went through as teammates and fellow coaches will be key to what we pass on to our players. I believe Joe and I are an extension of BSU and its blue-collar approach to football. Joe has been the catalyst of a lot of success that I have had, and not just me. There are other guys on the [Boise State] '94 team—DaWuan Miller, Rashid Gayle, Tim Foley. I could go down that roster and point out many other former teammates who were influenced by Joe in a positive manner.

"As a teammate and a fellow coach he was and has always been a standup guy. I don't care what happened in 2003. That's over. We all make mistakes. Joe O'Brien is a key reason why I have succeeded as a person and a coach."

Likewise.

During the Coyotes' training camp Biletnikoff and Smith asked me to stay with the team and serve as defensive line coach for the entire season, which ended in June. There were a number of good reasons *not* to accept their offer: It was still an unpaid position, I had my construction business to think about, and I missed Gracie terribly. If common sense had prevailed, I probably should have declined the offer and returned to Great Falls. Gracie had started her own photography business and didn't have the flexibility to drop everything and join me in Fresno; moreover, spring was upon us and Get The J.O'B Done had plenty of work in the offing. But my burning desire to get back into coaching overrode those concerns; I didn't know when or if another opportunity would come along. "Coaching is the truest, purest thing I've ever done in my life," I told Starks in the *Contra Costa Times*. "It's always been football, and I lost that. I thought it was over." With Gracie's blessing and my parole officer's OK, I made the necessary arrangements to have someone run my business for a few more months so I could remain with the Coyotes.

One reason I decided to stay was because of the connection I developed with the players and coaches, who accepted me for who I was, not what I had been. Like most coaching jobs, my position with Central Valley was a demanding, exhausting and time-consuming grind. But I had no complaints; I was in my element. "Re-entry to the game [is] his paycheck," Starks wrote. "The days are simple and repetitive in Fresno. O'Brien hops on Highway 41, makes the short jaunt to his office, heads to practice, and then returns to the apartment he shares with Smith."

"O'Brien gets a new beginning," wrote the *Statesman's* Prater, "a second chance to show his passion for coaching and prove his worth on a football field. 'This is everything to me,' I said in Prater's article. 'This is one of the very few things that makes me happy in life. I'm not going to give up on [a return to] coaching, that's for sure. This is just my first step of getting back into it.'"

Thankfully, I had Gracie's full support. "Gracie said her husband's pursuit of a coaching career is putting a financial burden on the family," wrote Prater, "not that it matters to either one of them. '[Joe] is so passionate about football—I don't even know if passionate is the word for it,' Gracie said in the same article. 'He wanted this so bad, and it's not like people are knocking down the door asking him to coach.'"

My lodging and a few free meals were the extent of my compensation. I even had to pay my own way to accompany the team on road trips, which I did willingly. One exception was when the Coyotes covered my airfare when they played a game in Pennsylvania so I could see my daughter, Haley, 11 at the time and living in Virginia with her mother.

Brian and Freddy said they hoped to eventually get me a salaried position with the coaching staff, but like many minor league franchises and leagues the Coyotes and af2 struggled financially, and the league folded after the 2009 season. Fred Biletnikoff Jr. and Brian Smith took a chance on me, for which I will always be grateful. Despite the demise of af2, my stint in Fresno had revitalized my coaching aspirations. Five months later, however, I was jolted back to reality.

THEY FLEW OUT of the Bobcat Stadium stands with equal malice. First came the taunts: "*DRUG ADDICT!*" "*TRAITOR!*" "*FELON!*" "*HYPO-CRITE!*" Then came the snowballs. Clearly directed at me, the jeers were scattered and the projectiles missed their mark as I stood on the sidelines that November afternoon in 2009 during the Sacramento State-Montana

State football game. But they hurt deeply nevertheless.

That humbling experience—my first appearance in a public venue in Bozeman since my arrest six years earlier and more than three years after my release from prison—served as a painful reminder that I remained an outcast in the eyes of many MSU followers.

My companions that day were former Bobcat players Jason Goodman and Adam Cordiero, a standout defensive end who played under me seven years earlier. We were the guests of then-Sac State assistant coach Willy Kofe, another one of my former players at MSU. We were on the sidelines near the Sacramento State bench to support Willy, with whom I have a close relationship. In fact, I went to the Hornets' game at Montana the previous season and stood on the sidelines—without incident—for the same reason.

With so much time having passed since my departure from MSU, I didn't expect much (if any) of a reaction to my appearance as I entered Bobcat Stadium. Still, I decided to play it safe and stood on the sidelines somewhat incognito, wearing Sacramento State gear and standing with my back to the crowd.

But once someone in the crowd recognized me in the first half, the invective and snowballs began flying. "Hey, we need to get out of here and not come back after halftime," said Adam. "It's dangerous out here. Someone's gonna get hurt."

"Go ahead," I replied, "but I ain't leaving."

We returned to our same spot in the second half and the insults and snowballs continued to fly. I knew it was a small percentage of the crowd that was doing the yelling and throwing, but it still hurt. The entire afternoon was an unpleasant reminder that my good intentions and a new lease on life weren't necessarily going to pave the way to widespread acceptance and forgiveness.

FOR 15 YEARS I made horrible choices and repeated blunders. I can never completely undo the damage I've done, but I can keep trying. One way is to tell my story so that others might avoid the same mistakes. Since my speech at Carroll College in April 2007 I've made similar presentations. In January 2009 I addressed a gathering of more than 130 college and high school student-athletes and coaches at the College of Southern Idaho, and six months later I spoke about my struggles with substance abuse to about 150 student-athletes at American River College at the invitation of my friend Jerry Haflich, the school's head football coach. I have also shared my story with the Great Falls Americans of the Northern Pacific Hockey League and a youth hockey team in Bozeman.

During those talks I mention the demons I have battled, but I don't dwell on them. Instead, I try to deliver a message that is uplifting and positive. When I talk to young people I tell them that sports is more than wins and losses. I tell them that athletics at its best breeds a physical confidence that can beget intellectual and spiritual grace. I tell them that teamwork is an indispensable ingredient to success, and it can help them deal with their individual flaws. If it seems appropriate, I tell them the Bible helped get me through prison and that my faith is what guides me today, but I don't go overboard. Faith—or the choice to be an unbeliever—is a deeply personal decision.

I believe faith and religion are individual choices. Gracie and I choose to be active in our church, Great Falls Christian Center, which has the second-largest congregation in Great Falls. In addition to our regular attendance at Sunday service, we are active in the church's youth ministry and participate in Bible studies. We go to a Christian couples group, and I have participated in a Christian men's breakfast group in Great Falls. I don't drink anymore, not even an occasional glass of wine. It's just a personal choice. I might have a glass of celebratory champagne if I coach on a team that wins a championship, but until then total abstinence is something that keeps me focused, grounded and headed in the direction that I need to go.

I GET IT. I know arena football is not the NFL. I know I'm chasing a dream that might seem improbable and out of reach. Even *without* a criminal record, I know landing an NFL coaching job is tough. I know my business might suffer because of my absence—but there will always be roofs to replace and buildings to repair. I'm only in my late 30s, which is young by coaching standards. But you can't move up the coaching ladder unless you're on the bottom rung at the very least. That's why I accepted Brian Smith's second offer to coach with him—this time with the 2011 Wenatchee Valley Venom of the Indoor Football League. But there were two important differences between my stints in Wenatchee and Fresno: This time I drew a salary and Gracie went with me.

I took the job with the Venom because coaching is my calling. I also took it because I believe in Brian Smith. He is a natural-born leader and a gifted football coach; he proved as much when took the Venom reins midway through the 2010 season after Keith Evans was fired as head coach. Playing in its inaugural season in the American Indoor Football League, Wenatchee Valley got off to a 2-5 start when the team's owners dismissed Evans in mid-May and promoted Brian from defensive coordinator to interim head coach.

A few days later Smith lost his head-coaching debut to San Jose 60-57 on a last-second field goal, but the Venom then reeled off six straight wins, finished 8-6, and fell just short of a playoff berth. During the team's late-season surge under Brian, the Wenatchee Valley brass decided to remove the interim tag from his title and named him head coach and general manager. Soon after his promotion, Brian called me about serving as the Venom's defensive coordinator in the revamped IFL—this time with pay.

"It wasn't a lot," said Smith of his salary offer, "but it was feasible enough to make Joe think about coming to Wenatchee for the season. From the beginning I had Joe in mind as my defensive coordinator. He is way overqualified to coach at Wenatchee, just like he was with the Coyotes in 2009. My selling point was that our defense would have a chance to learn from a very talented and passionate coach, and that he could, once again, get his foot in the door in the coaching profession. With his experience, discipline and intensity—all the stuff I believe in—I could not afford not to hire him. He has a love and a passion for the game that is unmatched."

My quest to revive my coaching career is important, but not as important as my marriage. As I pondered Brian's offer, I told Gracie I wouldn't accept it unless I had her unconditional backing. She has sacrificed a great deal for me already, and I was hesitant to put us through another lengthy separation. Moreover, the pay was hardly a major incentive—$700 per game with an additional $100 per win with bonuses for playoff berths and titles, plus housing.

I thought I might be asking too much. For two months Gracie and I discussed the emotional, financial and logistic pros and cons and prayed for guidance. In the fall of 2010 we finally decided that Gracie would accompany me to Wenatchee, and I agreed to Brian's offer to serve as the Venom's associate head coach/defensive coordinator/director of player personnel. Early in 2011 Gracie and I made the necessary arrangements to take care of our house and keep our respective businesses going, and, along with our dog, Kaliha, a 7½-year-old Weimaraner, we made the move 530 miles due west to the central Washington city of Wenatchee for the five-month IFL season.

I'M READY FOR the next chapters of my life. I'm genuinely excited for whatever is in store because the worst is certainly behind me. As long as I have God and Gracie I have the faith, strength and perseverance to forge ahead. Like any other human being I have my share of flaws and foibles, but I'd like to think that I'm a heckuva lot better person than I once was. The dark days of my past have given me a deep appreciation for life's many blessings.

I decided to write this book about my addiction and other personal struggles to help others learn from my mistakes. I don't want anyone to go through what I went through. I especially want to share my story with young adults who might be dealing with substance abuse or other demons. My message is simple: Whether it's through counseling, finding your faith, or simply going to someone who cares, there *are* solutions to seemingly hopeless situations. At various times I thought my circumstances were beyond help—that there was no escape from the despair, misery and loneliness I had inflicted on myself. I was wrong; there is a way out, and there's help for everyone. But you've got to ask.

I want to free myself from my past. But at the same time, I want to use that past to show that there are many avenues to renewal and redemption. For me, it began in prison when I became reacquainted with God. I talk to Him all the time. Because of Him I can handle anything that comes my way. I should have listened to Him a lot earlier.

But I sure am listening now.

About the Authors

JOE O'BRIEN grew up in Pittsburg, California, where he was a stand-out student and a three-sport star in high school. He played football at Santa Clara University and Boise State University. In 1994, his senior year at Boise State, he was a first-team Division 1-AA All-American defensive end and the Big Sky Defensive Player of the Year. He played pro football from 1995-98, including preseason stints with the NFL's Minnesota Vikings and New Orleans Saints. He earned a bachelor's degree from Boise State and worked as an assistant football coach at BSU, Northern Arizona and Montana State. In 2011 he joined the Wenatchee Valley Venom of the Indoor Football League as associate head coach/defensive coordinator/director of player personnel. He also owns a construction business in Great Falls, Montana, where he and his wife, Gracie, reside. His daughter, Haley, is in her early teens.

BOB EVANCHO has written three other books. He is the co-author of *Pokey: The Good Fight* and *Elegant Soul: The Life and Music of Gene Harris* as well as the writer/editor of *Ida Tours the 44: A Book of Idaho's Counties*. He was also a contributing writer/editor to three books published by Boise State University and has won numerous writing awards. Originally from Detroit, he received a bachelor's degree from Grand Valley State in Michigan and a master's degree from Boise State. He and his wife, Sue, live in Boise, Idaho. They have three children in their early 20s.